The Magic of *Words*

The Magic of Words

Write to Publish

A Collection of Short Stories and Poems

Write to Publish: A collection of short stories and poems.

Copyright 2018 by Write to Publish

All rights reserved. No part of this book may be reproduced in any manor whatsoever, or stored in any information system, without the prior written consent of the authors.

Publisher: Write to Publish

Printed in the United States of America

Books may be purchased through any of the Write to Publish Authors.

Cover and Interior design by: Write to Publish.
Photo by: iStock and WTP.
Editing: Will Allcorn, Carolyn Tody and Sherrie Fuscone

ISBN: 13:978-1985616714
ISBN: 10:1985616718

Dedicated
to
Dr. Randy Rassoul Johnston

Who has been and always will be an inspiration to the members of Write to Publish (WTP)

CONTENTS

Johnston, Randy... 1
   Executive.. 2
   Antoinette's Heart.................................... 4
   Lady Katherine....................................... 6
   Dreams of Paris...................................... 8
Allcorn, Will... 10
   Gotchya... 11
   There's a Monster in Our Midst............... 16
   Dr. Doom & the Chambers of Horror....... 22
Beroza, Jeanne.. 27
   Hard Year's Seasons-Haiku..................... 28
   The Wind... 29
   Circle of Life... 31
Brenner, Heather..................................... 37
   Special Olympics 2017........................... 38
Dowell, Betty... 43
   The Plucky Journey of Stacy.................. 44
   The Mighty Smudge.............................. 49
Filley, John... 57
   I'll Own You Then Kill You..................... 58
   Always Half Awake............................... 60
   Worse Than Hell................................... 63
Fuscone, Sherrie..................................... 68
   David and the Injured Gosling................ 69
   Mrs. Chutney's Eulogy.......................... 76
   The Extra Child..................................... 84
Hebert, Yvonne....................................... 91
   Forgiveness and Trust............................ 92
   The Potty Box Standoff......................... 95
Helton, Della... 98
   Blueberry Picking................................. 100

Hoard, Peggy 102
  The Case 103
  Does She Know I Care 106
  A Twinkle in His Eye 109
  The Honor of Veterans 115

Link, Jerry 117
  2017 Total Solar Eclipse 119
  Pruning Apple Trees 125

Markham, Patricia 128
  Beach Musing 129
  Looking for Jesus 130
  Untitled 131
  His Heart in Me 132
  The Winter of Lack 133
  The Winter of Plenty 135

Smith, Ray 137
  Not to Baltimore 138
  Outside the Box 141

Tody, Carolyn 146
  Evolutionary Change 147
  Guardian 149
  Tristan 150
  The Old Storyteller 156

Waller, Betty 163
  Five Faces of Fear 164
  Royalty in the Classroom 171

Whetter, Tom 178
  Sorry, Wrong Number 179
  Hair Brush 182
  My Brothers and Me 191

ACKNOWLEDGEMENTS

It is through the leadership of Peggy Hoard that this book was made possible.

Peggy and Will Allcorn have spent countless hours organizing, typing, proofing and then loading the contents into Create Space. Those of us who were fortunate enough to have some of our works printed between these covers sincerely thank them.

We thank Tom Whetter for the book's title. He only had to mention *THE MAGIC OF WORDS* once and we knew it would be the one.

For the cover design we thank John Filley for showing us how to find designs and Will Allcorn for searching the web to discover it. We thank iStock for the photo and both Will Allcorn and Peggy Hoard for tweaking the photo with various titles of the works within. The choice was the perfect companion for the title.

Sherrie Fuscone, Carolyn Tody and Will Allcorn spent many hours editing the submissions and we greatly thank them for their time.

We thank Will Allcorn, Peggy Hoard and Linda Elsroad for the tedious hours spent meticulously pouring over the proofs.

We thank Patricia Markham for solving technical issues, enabling us to proceed with uploading our book into Create Space.

To the entire WTP (Write to Publish) group, both past and present, we thank you. It is your collective imaginations, knowledge and encouragement that fill these pages.

We also wish to thank those who sit quietly (and for the most part patiently) in the background: **our families and friends.**

And last, but not least, we are very grateful for Create Space, a wonderful platform for those writers who would never get their creations into print otherwise.

INTRODUCTION

Write to Publish - WTP is a group of writers connected by the need to express ourselves through writing. WTP provides the framework that enables individual expression by sharing our skills and artistic craft with others in an atmosphere that is fun and enriching.

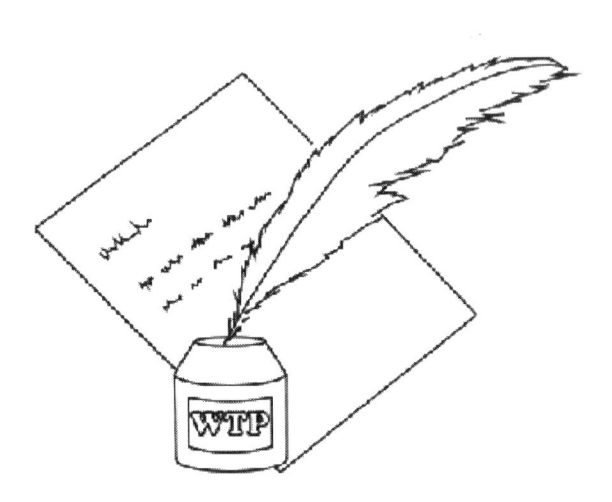

Our Mission Statement defines what we do and what we wish to share with our community.

"We gather to inspire and share original works of writing. As published or unpublished writers, our goal is to publish. We learn from each other. We promote and sponsor guests, writers and speakers to Cadillac to enhance our writing art and that of the community. Our guiding behaviors include support and critique in an open, fun, honest and respectful manner."

Dr. Randy Rassoul Johnston was born in Toledo, Ohio. ~~After graduating high school she attended~~ and graduated from Toledo University. She then attended Middlebury College in Massachusetts for a year. Pursuing her dream, she traveled to Paris, France to attend the Sorbonne and studied French language and literature.

Upon returning to the United States, Randy taught at Ottawa Hills, then Ada, Ohio. After that she continued to teach at Lock Haven, Pennsylvania. Deciding she wanted to obtain her doctorate she taught and attended the University of Michigan, obtaining a doctorate in French language and literature. (She was also fluent in Spanish.)

Wanting to change direction she left teaching and opened her own travel agency, Metavoyage. She helped many people achieve their dreams of traveling to Europe, Britain and Ireland.

While living in Ann Arbor she purchased a little cabin overlooking the Middle Branch River in Marion, Michigan. Many weekends were spent in the country, a rest from the bustle of city life. She met the love of her life, Jack. After marriage she sold her condo and they moved to the cabin. Jack added the *river room,* increasing the living space.

It was here that Randy spent two years writing her travel book, *I Slept in a Pineapple*. It is a complete travel guide with breath taking photos, detailed descriptions, maps and complete work sheets.

Jack, her "Knight in shinning armor," enabled her to live an enchanted life in their little cabin, until her death in July, 2017

Executive

I began that fateful day as I had so many others, still unbelieving that I was walking the ancient streets of Paris, eager as so many had been before to learn in the historic halls of the Sorbonne.

On certain days, when my soul aligned perfectly with the rhythms of the city, the sounds of long ago came to me in Latin. And so connected was I to all those who came before me, that it was not strange. And although I did not understand the words, I understood the message sent to me from scholars far away in time. For we were soul mates, imprisoned together willingly in the conquests of Paris. I understood that one day my words would join theirs and whisper through the years to those who would come after me.

After class, what else but sit at a cafe with a *chocolat* and *croissant*? Paris spread out before me, reading the great masterpieces of French literature, preparing for the next class, hoping to gain insights into the source of artistic inspiration and beauty.

All my dreams had come true, except one, and Paris knew it was missing. She had seen my glancing at the lovers walking along the *grand boulevards* and narrow alleys arm in arm. The *River Seine* had told her how I watched them embrace in the protective shadows of her bridges.

Paris owned my soul, and thrilled the depths of my spirit. She had planted the rose of romance in my heart so I would long for a lover's touch on my hand, and yearn to be embraced along the *Seine.*

When that happened, every facet of my being would be under her control. Supremely she exerted her secret strategics, planning each subtle moment, to give me every pleasure of mind and soul. And, at last, the roman tic love that only she could grant, the unforgettable experience of being young and in love in Paris.

Antoinette's Heart

Dr. Martell dismounted, and slumped against the great horse's flank. His mind and muscles unresponsive, beaten and wounded by the grim round of dawn to dusk patient visits, from the wretched routine of infection, lesions, phlegm and malignancies.

His manservant took the reins. The horse's hooves clopped quietly on the cobblestones, stepping slowly, more slowly, more slowly still, willing itself to reach the stable. All the strength was sapped from the giant muscles that carried the man on paths without end to remote farms, villages and homes where human decline and decay dwelled.

"Thank you, Stevens," said the doctor. Drained, he urged his listless limbs to carry him to home and hearth.

Martha opened the door and curtsied. The house was quiet. Again the drawing room was empty. Antoinette, his young wife, was not there to take tea with him. He loved to ease his weariness by looking at her delicate features, dark hair, slim figure and elegant dress. With her, instantly the numbing monotony of a country doctor's life vanished.

She came only rarely these days to take tea with him. He sensed her disdain for his rough boots. He sensed her disdain for his dusty jacket, disdain for his dull conversation.

In the kitchen, he sipped hot tea and sampled Marthas scones.

"Is Mrs. Martell at home?" he asked.

"Yes," Martha replied, "she has spent the afternoon in her boudoir."

The word "boudoir" echoed like a thousand screams in his ears. He didn't want to look, but perverse curiosity prevailed and he stared at the kitchen counter. There, like thieves, greedy invoices and unpaid bills vied for his attention.

Waves of weariness and defeat struck him. He would never be the husband of Antoinette's heart. She lived in a dream world of lust — lust for art, music, fine china and silver, refined ladies and gentlemen, elegant conversations — and without thought, she brought them to the brink of bankruptcy, creating in her boudoir a haven of luxury, a fitting retreat, to shield herself from him and the coarse existence she loathed.

Lady Katherine

The scene on the TV screen brought fury, hatred — an eruption of violent uncontrollable rage — bordering on madness — to the depth of Ruth's soul.

She listened, her face contorted with wrath.

"Jonathan Randolph, Britain's premier symphony orchestra conductor, stood before Queen Elizabeth today in Buckingham Palace and was knighted," the newscaster announced. "At his side was Katherine, his wife, Lady Katherine as she is now referred to. She herself is very accomplished. Lady Katherine is one of Britain's most talented photographers with frequent exhibitions around the world. The power couple live in London's fashionable Mayfair district."

"Tell me, Lady Katherine," the newscaster asked, "how does it feel to have your husband receive one of the highest honors that Britain can bestow?"

Ruth did not hear Katherine's reply. The bitterness she felt towards her former husband and his new wife filled her mind with loathing that blocked any ability to focus.

Only the words Lady Katherine Randolph rang in her brain. "Lady Katherine, how dare you," Ruth screamed at the TV.

"You bitch, you whore, I am Lady Randolph. You are an unallowable aberration in my life!"

Then Ruth became calm, and a deadly smile came onto her face. "Retribution, vengeance, justice, they will all be mine!" Still smiling, she reviewed the fatal plan in her mind.

She leafed through a magazine, pouring once again over the article about Katherine and her photographic techniques, how she developed all her own film in the World War II bomb shelter that remained on the property of the Mayfair townhouse.

The TV interview provoked Ruth to implement the plan tonight. She made her way to Mayfair, crept silently to the bomb shelter, and while Katherine worked inside developing photos, Ruth quietly closed the ventilator cap on top and placed an iron wedge through the door handle mechanism.

No cell phone signal in a sealed shelter, of course. The only thing Ruth regretted about her plan was that she would have to be satisfied with imaging the desperate screams and pleas for help from Katherine as she ran out of air, gasping, choking, convulsing as she died a horrible death. No scream could penetrate the massive walls of the shelter. Neither Ruth nor anyone else would hear a sound.

A pity I can't enjoy listening to her agony, thought Ruth. *Oh well, I have a great imagination.....*

Dreams of Paris

   Recollections of my college days are separate from the great storehouse of memories jumbled together from the rest of my life. They are radiant images of four years unlike any that had come before, never to be repeated or recaptured.
   The traditional rhythm of college life begins with enjoying dances and parties during the first two years, dating different people and lots of group activities - followed by gradually discovering who that one special person might be.
  This happens during the junior year - the pairing off of couples who date only each other, and with stars in their eyes, they fall in love. This brings its own stream of special occasions - pinning parties, for the Greeks on campus - that is, those of us who belonged to sororities and fraternities.
   I was a member of Zeta Tau Alpha sorority, and we were linked closely to the guys in Sigma Phi Epsilon fraternity - the Sig Eps, as they were called. My big sister in my sorority is a good example. During her Junior year, she began to seriously date one of the Sig Eps, and the next step in the relationship was to get pinned. The guy would ask the girl to be his one and only, and if she accepted, he gave her his fraternity pin which she wore along side her sorority pin. They were pinned - and at a special party, all the Sig Eps would come and serenade the newly pinned couple.
   The pinned couples usually got formally engaged late in their Junior year or early in their Senior year. This brought more parties and oohing and aahing over sparkling engagement rings.
   Starting in my Freshman year, in May, I delighted in the stream of wedding announcements of my friends,

especially my sorority sisters, who were Seniors and marrying their college sweethearts.

Spring and early summer brought a flurry of graduation parties, bridal showers, and June weddings.

But not for me. I did not get pinned, nor engaged. I had some big crushes on guys in college - but it never developed beyond that - because I was already hopelessly in love - with dreams or Paris - and my parents had agreed that after graduation I could spend a year studying there.

When I arrived in Paris, like countless students before me who walked her ancient streets, my soul belonged to her. She beguiled me, binding me tightly to her. Proudly she displayed her majestic monuments, grand boulevards, hidden squares, sparkling fountains, and elegant facades.

Paris claimed my young girl's mind and soul, vowing one day that I would walk arm in arm along the Seine River with my first love. She would bestow upon me the ultimate emotion, first love in Paris. She kept her promise, and nothing will ever be as sublime as romantic embraces in the protective shadows of the bridges along the Seine. Memories of being young and in love in Paris - rare memories of perfection never to be equalled.

William L. Allcorn joined his first book club at the young age of seven, *Golden Dog* was the title, and he was hooked. From that day forward every allowance, whatever extra money he could earn doing small yard jobs, it all went towards his monthly selection. As the years passed his personal library grew.

Being the avid reader Will was, he'd always wondered what it would be like to write his own book. For years he had been doing all the art work, and wrote the prose for greeting cards, but a novel seemed out of question.

Then it was time, the first couple of attempts were rough, raw. Then, persuaded to join a writer's group, (the WTP), Will quickly saw the wealth of experience from which he could learn. He learns from them yet today.

Will has a trilogy part one ready for print which should be coming out soon.

You are a great addition to our group

Will Allcorn

Gotchya

Henry peeked through the crack in the bedroom door to make sure Beth, his wife, was still asleep. Like usual she had pulled the blanket up and was buried beneath its folds, but the resounding snore was all he needed for proof. As quiet as a church mouse he tippy toed through the house. Dressed entirely in black he was all but invisible as he moved through the darkened rooms. At the front door he stopped and cocked his head, was that his name he heard? No, it was just his overwrought nerves. He slipped outside and went directly to his car.

He was thankful for the Prius as he backed down the driveway. The electric motor silently propelled the small car to the street. It was only four miles to his destination and at this time of the morning he drove virtually unseen along the deserted avenue. Even so he watched as lights began to appear in some of the windows, announcing that others were also beginning to rouse. He only hoped he hadn't left too late. If he was seen, his well thought out plans would fail to come to fruition.

The First Baptist Church was just ahead on the left. He pulled into Meijer's parking lot across the street. There were only a handful of cars at the far end and he assumed these belonged to the stores employees. Avoiding the bright lights of the lot he walked along the weed choked ditch to a forested area adjacent to the church. It was there that he would lie in wait.

A tinge of orange had just started to color the eastern skyline when he arrived at the footbridge. He pressed the button on the side of his watch and a soft blue glow illuminated the dial. Goofy stared up at him with a silly leer on his face and his gloved hands pointing out the time. 7:00 a.m.

Panting from the exertion he berated himself for having that second helping of mashed potatoes and gravy at dinner the evening before, let alone two scoops of vanilla ice cream with his pie.

"I swear, starting tomorrow I'm going on a diet." Henry patted the bulge at his midriff.

A pair of headlights pulled into the church's parking area followed by another and another. He crouched beside the wooden structure and peered through the stand of withered cattails which grew every summer along this end of the gully. Several adults emerged from their cars and joined together. A short elderly man started giving orders and pointing this way and that way.

One of the group turned and it seemed like he was looking in his direction. Henry subconsciously ducked even lower and then chuckled. Dressed as he was he knew the likelihood of him being seen was close to nil. Still, if he was spotted it would ruin everything. He'd been meticulously planning this attack for weeks and had no intention of letting his eagerness spoil it now.

It was dry under the bridge and would be until the spring rains started. After making himself a comfortable nest he closed his eyes, only intending to take a short nap while he could. Slowly his head nodded two or three times before he drifted off into a deeper slumber than he would've liked.

It was the shrill cries of children playing in the distance that roused him and his eyes snapped open. A slow evil smile crossed his weathered face; the children had been set loose to join in the annual Easter egg hunt. He reached into his satchel and withdrew the mask he'd brought along to conceal his identity.

He was going to have to be more alert; she would eventually come to this ravine. For several weeks he'd been watching her play after church services were over and knew she seemed to favor this section of Avalon's small municipal park. His only concern was that she would bring a friend, but this was an event where it was every child for him or herself and he told himself he was being foolish. She would come alone.

If this was going to work he was going to have to act fast. He wanted to get this part of the trap set as soon as the adults were finished hiding the holiday treats, but it was too late for that. He slipped from beneath the bridge and went directly to the edge of the nearby clearing. From his satchel he scattered a handful of chocolate bunnies, the hollow ones, these were her favorites.

As he walked back to his hiding spot he strategically placed several more along the way. Knowing her tenacity he was satisfied they would lead her to his "lair" and then, if everything went as planned, right into his clutches. The thought thrilled him and his smile deepened,

Ssh. What was that? The elderly man cocked his head listening for the slight rustle to repeat itself. Suddenly a gray squirrel scampered across his field of vision, an acorn from a nearby oak tree held tightly in its mouth. After he sat back again he noticed his heart was beating fast and hard. Was it because the little animal had startled him, or was it because he thought it was her?

The dry, brittle spring leaves crunched again, but this time he was sure the sound was caused by a footstep. There was a pause, then another footstep, followed by another and another. It wouldn't do to come out of hiding and have it be one of the adults, or worse yet Bill Ryan, the local police officer, walking his beat through the park.

There was more movement followed by another pause. He was positive that the light footsteps were hers. When the next pause came he mentally conjured up an image of her slight form as she bent to pick up yet another piece of the bait. His well devised trap was going along as scheduled, and without a hitch.

His heart beat ever faster.

"Sally……Sally," a woman's voice called out from the church parking lot.

Dammit, I can't be cheated of my prize now, not after all the time and effort I've put into getting her alone. And she's so close, it's just not fair, Henry scowled.

"I'll be there in a minute Mommy," the young girl yelled back, hoping she'd be able to hear her. "I found some of my special bunnies."

"What did you say sweetie? Mommy can barely hear you."

"I'll be right there," Sally yelled a little louder.

"Okay, just don't wander too far…in fact why don't you come a little closer where Mommy can keep an eye on you?"

Sally spotted more candy at the edge of the ditch and mumbled, "Just let me get these last few bunnies."

Henry backed deeper into the shadows. There were several footsteps. She'd scrambled down the small slope and was on the floor of the gully itself. Henry started to sweat beneath his mask.

There was another footstep. He could now see her pink dress through the brown cattails and trembled with anticipation. Another step. Just two more steps and she'd be within striking distance. Another step.

A gloved hand started to reach menacingly out of the gloom.

"Sally….Sally, where are you sweetie? Mommy can't see you."

"I'm here Mo…." A small twig snapped behind her and she whirled around.

"Gotchya!"

Henry took off the Easter Bunny mask. "How'd ya know?"

"You'll have to do better than that if you want to catch me Grandpa. After all, you're the one who taught me everything I know about winning the game of Gotchya."

"Yeah, well I'm gonna teach you a new game called *I'm Gonna Getchya.*"

Henry wiggled his fingers and then chased her all the way back to the church, bellowing out fearsome threats of a severe tickling.

There's a Monster in Our Midst

The last thing the creature remembered was several of the Masters coming into her pen, each of them carrying one of the hated glow sticks. Never before had she seen them burn so hotly. Her bushy tail had whipped back and forth in agitation. Then came the biting jolt of electricity. Fighting through the intense pain she was rewarded with the feel of tearing flesh as she reached out a raking claw. At lease one of her assailants would go down with her. Then the darkness came.

It was the raucous clamor which finally roused her. She lay there listening for several seconds when suddenly she realized the ground was cold. Cold? The temperature inside her pen never changed. For a brief moment she thought she was dreaming of home when a sharp stick poked her in the ribs. Startled, she jumped to a standing position; surrounding her was a world blanketed in white.

Last night when the Masters had come in to stun her she had been aboard one of their dreaded ships. Where had they left her? Where was she?

The raucous noise was repeated. Sitting in the branches of a nearby tree a blue jay called out to the world that there was a monster into our midst. Her stomach growled, so she picked up a stout cudgel and threw it with deadly accuracy. Like a stone the dazed bird fell into her waiting grasp. The meal was over quickly. As she sat spitting out a couple of loose feathers, her stomach growled again.

Her four hundred pound frame required no less than twenty pounds of meat daily; the small bird was a paltry meal at best. She would have to hunt. In the confines of her enclosure the Masters had always provided her with plenty of meat. Weekly they would release one of the grass eaters that roamed her world in vast, countless herds. But the ones raised on the ship were lethargic, stupid, and easy to kill.

Before her capture she was considered one of the great hunters of her pack. And oh how she loved to hunt, the wind rushing through her fur when the chase was on. The smell of fear when the prey knew death was imminent.

The smell here is different, somewhat acidic, but even that is an intoxicating change to the stale, recycled air she had been breathing. No matter which direction she looked there were trees of every description. Compared to the lofty giants of her world these were smaller, like a forest of new growth after a burn.

The little winged creatures, which flitted about the tangle of their branches, were covered in feathers rather than leathery hide. She'd hunt them for food only if she had to. They'd be hard to catch and would require a lot of energy in the process. Surely there'd be larger game on this world, so without further hesitation she dropped to all fours and set off at a leisurely lope in search of her next meal. Heavy webbing between the fingers of both her hands and her 'hants,' or hand-feet, kept her from floundering in the powdery snow.

For miles she traveled without slowing when suddenly a burst of annoying, harsh noise echoed through the trees. It was an unnatural sound and she stopped. Her long pointed ears swiveled this way and that way as they sought to locate the source. Another voice chimed in and then a third. They were faint, but she was sure the chatter came from some form of larger animals. There was prey nearby.

Moving into the shadows she wound her way cautiously through the trees. The voices continued to grow steadily clearer with every passing footstep. Fifteen minutes later, from the lee of a fallen evergreen, she was looki down into a narrow gully.

At the bottom three figures sat huddled around a blazing fire. They had a strange resemblance to the Masters and she snarled in anger. At second glance it was obvious the similarity ended there, these humanoids had hair on their heads and faces. Still, the semblance was enough to raise the hackles on her shoulders; whoever they were, they would not capture her again. They were conversing in a guttural language and she moved closer to listen.

"I remember a time back in sixty-four when me and Harry Donaldson, you guys remember him don't cha? Well anyways, we was huntin' for this big buck we'd been hearing rumors about. It was up across the Mighty Mac, somewhere near the village of Calderwood. Huntin' hadn't been none too good so we went to this redneck bar called 'The Last Chance Saloon'….."

When the old man saw their knowing smiles he quickly added, "To shake off the chill."

After a burst of laughter he continued: "Any ways, while we was doin' just that we overheard some of the locals jawing about this twenty-four pointer running the swamp south of town."

"A twenty-four pointer!" the man sitting across from him said in pretended awe, and then nudged the man to his right. "Last time old Charlie told this tale it was only a twenty pointer."

Charlie ignored the interruption and continued, "Well, Harry an' me, we decided we was gonna be the ones to bag that there big buck. So's I packed up that old fifty caliber with as much powder as she'd hold and headed into the woods."

The bottle of inexpensive brandy was handed to him, he stopped his narrative to take a hearty swig.

"Isn't that the same gun there Grandpa?" a young boy who had just entered the scene asked, his eyes wide with adoration.

"It's not a gun Bobby, it's a rifle." The man across from Charlie frowned at his son.

"I meant rifle."

"If yer gonna start huntin' with us yer gonna have to know yer weapon."

"I'm tryin' Dad." The boy hung his head, a ruddy glow coloring his cheeks.

"Where was I now? Oh yeah" Charlie, the eldest passed the bottle along. "We'd been walkin' the woods all day, keepin' ta the high ridges, when about dusk, I seen this buck leave the protection of the cedars. I swear, it had a rack this wide!" He put his hands out in front of him, greatly exaggerating the width.

"How far away was it Grandpa?"

"Prit'near four hundred yards, and a fair wind was blowin' too!"

The two men sitting across from the older gentleman snickered, and then each of them took a pull on the bottle before handing it back to him, who in turn handed it to his grandson.

"I really don't think I should Grandpa." The fifteen-year old sneaked a quick look at his father and then turned back to the old man. "I've never had alcohol before."

"If he's gonna come huntin'....." Charlie eyed the boy's father.

"Okay, go ahead Bobby, just don't let yer mother find out." He stood and put a loving hand on his son's shoulder. "Besides, it's become kind of a tradition for everyone to have a drink, you know, to celebrate the first kill of the season."

Bobby gingerly accepted the bottle, and emulating his grandfather, took a lengthy gulp. Half of it sprayed across the snow as he coughed and sputtered.

All three of the adults laughed and clapped the newest member of the group on the back.

"Bobby, you're truly one of us now."

The young man beamed at his new-found recognition, and as soon as he was done choking asked, "so, did you get the deer Grandpa?"

"Sure'nuff did. One shot." The old man's gaze seemed to wander to a time long past and a wistful smile crossed his face. "Yes sir, one shot, right through the heart and it went down where it stood. Best shot I ever made. Hell, best shot I ever seen!"

The young female looked down upon the group with contempt. They were noisy and they reeked of the liquid they were consuming so freely. Then the slight breeze brought a new scent to her attention. Moving to a better advantage she espied the buck hanging on the far side of a sturdy oak tree. Blood oozed from the open cavity to coagulate on the gore littered snow beneath. This animal had a familiar smell, reminding her of a tasty herbivore she'd hunted many times in the forests of her home world. Drool spilt from beneath the three inch canines.

She watched the three larger males for a couple of minutes and came to the conclusion that physically they would be no match against her greater strength. Her scrutiny shifted, she was armed with razor sharp claws and fangs, but leaning against a tree several feet away from them were sticks, not unlike those the Masters had. Even though these were not quite the same, she was certain they could inflict a serious injury. She would have to take the group by surprise.

Using their loud banter to her advantage she stealthily inched her way down the steep slope. Once she was within striking distance she stopped only long enough to make sure the situation hadn't changed. There was little to fear, their weapons were still out of reach.

With a roar meant to temporarily paralyze, she leapt among them, and all hell broke loose. She raked the nearest of them across the side of his head, leaving an ear and good potion of his scalp to hang limply on his shoulder. Her rush continued.

The laughter died on the boy's lips as his father's blood splattered across his face. He fell backwards. Reflexively he threw out his arms to break his fall, burying his hands to the wrists in the fiery coals of the campfire. Consumed with anguish he never saw the massive wolf-like figure step over him.

She had the second male held high over her head with the intention of snapping his spine when she noticed the third, the eldest, leveling one of the strange-looking sticks in her direction. Muscles bunched beneath her thick brindle coat. She hurled her burden full in the face of the man with the puny weapon. Together they went down in a tangled heap. Never stopping she was upon them, tearing, slashing, biting.

Screaming, the boy rolled from the shattered embers. His hands blistered and badly charred.

Turning her attention away from the three mangled and dying males she leapt upon the writhing youth and buried her fangs deep into the back of his neck. Violently she shook him until she heard the tell-tale snap of parting vertebrae. Satisfied he was dead, she dropped the twitching corpse to the snow and then stood upon it, roaring forth her victory to the heavens.

With the humanoids no longer a threat she walked over to where the fine young herbivore, a five pointer, hung suspended by a heavy rope. It was a small matter to chew through it and then she slung the meaty animal over her massive shoulder.

Leaving the scene of carnage without so much as a backwards glance she strode into the trees, secure in the knowledge that tonight she would feed.

Through the Eyes of a Child
aka
Dr. Doom and the Chamber of Horrors

I stare numbly out the rain-splattered window of the car; it's dismal, and the low, gray clouds have devoured any and all sign of the sun. It's fitting though; I've been dreading this day for two weeks, ever since Dr. Sawsall called me on the phone to give me the results of the biopsy. I was originally referred to him because the alien thing attached to my finger was growing. For years it lay in wait, quiet and benign, then ***boom!*** In a matter of months the ugly fiend has managed to bury its roots bone-deep and is now in the process of devouring my flesh at an alarming rate. Yep, today is the day Dr. Sawsall says it has to go.

Thinking back to the day of the biopsy I cringe. The day Dr. Sawsall, or Dr. Doom, as I've referred to him ever since, filleted my finger in a manner not unlike my Uncle Barney cleaning fish. ***Ouch***!

Dr. Doom tried to explain to me that he required such an enormous slab of meat to send in for testing. Even then I remember him as cold, heartless, and one would even say, diabolical.

I also remember that first trip to his office taking a bazillion years to get here, but today every mile seemed to go by in two blinks of an eye and the twitch of the nose.

At the entrance I balk, but my companion, always a bully when it comes to my well being, pushes me into the waiting room. Everyone looks up. Has word of this alien creature gotten out? No, there's a look of empathy in their eyes which tells me they've been where I'm going. Yet, I'm no amateur, I've already walked through the green door, and lived to talk about it. Who am I trying to kid? I'm really quite nervous; this is no mere slab of meat Dr. Doom is going to remove today. He's going for the whole enchilada!

I try to read one of those woman's magazines, the ones which are piled helter-skelter on the corner table in every doctor's office, but I'm reading the same paragraph for the third time. Even the pages upon pages of recipes with their scrumptious photos don't cause me to drool like they usually do. They simply remind me of the last meal a condemned man gets before he stands in front of a firing squad.

The hushed talk in the waiting room is silenced as a woman's contralto voice rolls over it like thunder: "Tommy, Tommy Christmas!"

I stand and everyone stares in my direction.

The woman beckons for me and my friend to pass beyond the green door. She closes it behind us and I could swear I hear the click of a pin sliding into place. Like sheep we're herded through a maze of corridors. I'm sure the layout was designed to confuse and dumbfound any escapee.

At room 666 she stops, it's a bad omen. I stand there wondering what I've gotten myself into when the door swings open of its own violation. Once inside she sits me in the 'hot seat' and motions for my companion to take one of the spectator's chairs. Before leaving she assures me: "Nurse Williams will be with you shortly."

Preoccupied over what's to come I'm barely aware of my surroundings. Then I hear the door swoosh open. I look up from my musings and the first thing I notice is the woman's immense size. She's easily eight feet tall.

My eyes are drawn to the tray in her hands and I blanch. Covering its stainless steel surface are numerous instruments used to cause intense anguish. At the counter she turns and a smile crosses her face, she opted for just the perfect implement to start things off.

I squeeze my eyes tight and turn away, I can't watch. Strange that I should think of it with everything going on, but I'm sure Sandy, my cohort and driver, is scrutinizing every move the nurse makes, her nose only inches away should she miss any of the action.

"Mr. Christmas, I want you to know it's nothing personal, but this is really gonna hurt."

Sandy's grinning, I just know it. She says it's a nervous condition, but I wonder, does she secretly get some kind of morbid fascination out of seeing others suffer? Then my hand is suddenly in the grip of something subhuman! I open my eyes, just a little, to see if maybe 'The Incredible Hulk' had made a guest appearance. They widen in horror as 'The Amazon' plunges five inches of hypodermic needle into the side of my finger. OMG! My toes curl from the pain. I would jump off the table here and now but for the 'Amazon's' iron clad grasp. Six, seven more times she drives the dripping point into me like some yellow jacket gone mad.

"Is your finger dead yet?"

Dead? Did she say *dead*?

The 'Amazon' seemed to take pleasure out of pushing the point of some knife like object into the area just behind my cuticle. Thankfully all sense has already left my finger.

Now its time for the real master of torment to make his appearance. The door opens right on cue.

There's a glimmer in his eye which says he's fanatical about his job and I nervously greet him, "Hello Doctor Sawsall. Today's the day, eh?"

"Hehehe, so it is, so it is." He depresses the button on the light saber in his hand. **Zzzitt!** Time to look away.

Even dead my finger feels the heat, but I quickly realize it really doesn't hurt. Then the acrid smell of burning flesh assails my nostrils and in mere seconds the stench becomes overpowering. For some God forsaken reason I get the urge to sneak a peak and immediately regret it.

The laser's blue beam cuts cleaner than any scalpel, and it nauseates me to watch my finger being peeled like an onion. A shudder racks my stiffened frame and my eyes involuntarily snap shut. But not before I get a quick glance of 'Amazon' handing her master a rasp-like tool. Her grip tightens; a vise couldn't hold my hand any more securely. I can almost feel the charred flesh ripping away as he draws the coarse tool back and forth.

"Is there no bottom to the roots on this little devil?"

What's that he mumbled?

For another thirty minutes I go through the process of burn and scrape, burn and scrape. There's a pause and I sigh. He's *finally* done.

"Nurse Williams," the maniacal leer on Dr. Sawsall face deepens, "turn his finger over. I want to mangle the other side also."

My sigh quickly turns into a moan.

She wrenches my finger around like it belongs to 'Stretch Armstrong.' Once again I'm thankful for the anesthetic. The searing of flesh begins anew. Finally Dr. Doom is finished and the 'Amazon' dabs away a droplet of sweat from his brow. As if he had something to sweat about!

At the door he turns, "Nurse Williams, you know what to do."

He doesn't even say goodbye as he shuts the heavy iron door behind himself, he simply moves on to his next victim.

"Let's cauterize this wound before you bleed to death. 'Old Sparky,' the nickname she calls the laser, flashes to life.

Here we go again! More burning and smoke and then its over, I will not bleed to death. The instant she releases my finger it beings to swell, even so she dresses the wound, and I can feel the bandaging grow steadily tighter.

After everything is all said and done, my driver and I are shown to the exit. On the way home the sky looks a little brighter. I have survived *"Dr. Doom and the Chamber of Horrors."*

Jeanne Beroza is a native of Michigan. She now lives in the Black Hills of South Dakota with her husband, horses, a cat and two Alaskan Malamutes. She is no longer working for Search and Rescue with her dogs, fighting fires or serving as a volunteer EMT for Custer County.

Now retired, she spends her time hiking with her dogs, riding horses, working on her pine needle art and writing. Jeanne loves nature and above all else, animals. 'The Nature of everything' is the fodder for her keyboard.

HARD YEAR'S SEASONS - HAIKU 8/2015, JTB

Starved carcass roadside
Victim of record winter
Tummies bulge, new life

Back from grey
Spring breeze soothes raw skin
Souls fly free

Nature heals
A twisted wire soul
Summer's song

In death, colors blaze
Antlers clash to start new life
Approaching winter

Colored lights, mall throng
White death buries weak and weary
Solstice logs burn high

The Wind

Well fed and sated from a long winter of snow, ice and cloud filled skies, masses of cold air lay over the deep blue waters of Lake Michigan. Sluggish and reluctant to move, they hug the water like bloated, opaque caterpillars eating the cold, growing bigger and heavier.

Along the Manistee lakeshore an early spring sun shines weakly, warming sandy beaches and causing flies to hatch in sheltered dune grasses. A family has traveled to the beach today, happy that winter has finally come to an end. The young mother sits on a towel and wears a light nylon jacket. Her legs are bare. She wishes the sun were a little warmer. She'd like to soak up a few rays to start an early season tan. The father is playing catch the Frisbee with the family's Golden Retriever. He's already working up a light sweat, while nearby, his small son and daughter wade into the shallow water at the lake's edge.

"Don't go in too far," yells the mother, not understanding her children are in no danger of doing such a thing since even the slow, shallow waves washing lazily ashore are ice cold and numbing. The children scream and dance as they dash in and out, getting wet only to their ankles.

The dog barks and runs back and forth from the water's edge, biting at the foam of the small waves lapping the sand at the childrens feet, to further up the groomed sand beach to where the man throws the Frisbee and yells, "Catch it Rowdy, catch it!"

By early afternoon the sun has risen higher in the sky and has begun to warm the sand and the air just above it. Mom removes her jacket to lather on suntan lotion. Feeling the water lose some of it bite, both children start venturing out deep enough to wet their shins. The man stops throwing the Frisbee to grab a drink of water and take refreshment from a basket sitting on a nearby picnic table.

Rowdy barks with joy and runs across the sand to lunge into the water where the children play. Laughing, the small boy throws a ball out into the waves. The dog swims after it getting wet all over, brings it back to drop at the boy's feet and then shakes, wetting both children thoroughly.

"Mom, mom, its cold," the children scream and scamper back to her, teeth chattering, arms covered in goose bumps, as they beg for towels and warmth. A breeze begins to blow off the lake bringing with it cooler air that causes the children to huddle together under mom's beach towel. She's put her jacket back on and is trying to wipe off the sand the children kicked onto her lotion-covered legs off with a corner of the towel.

Dad, now refreshed, resumes tossing the Frisbee for the dog. "Come play with us," he calls to his kids, "moving will keep you warm until the sun heats the water more."

Out over the lake, the caterpillar of cold air laughs at the family. It is only early spring, he thinks. The water in this big, deep lake is still very cold. Shine, sun, shine! Warm the shallows so the spring breeze dances and spins, mixing the water until cold begins to flow onshore. Then I can move. "I am bored," he rumbles." A little more sun and I will stream under the wings of seagulls. I will rustle new leaves forming on trees in the park and I will send the debris of winter swirling against fence rows. Those who thought I wouldn't move today will shiver and seek warmth indoors. I am the wind and I am just waiting for a burst of sunshine to warm the Earth so I can flow!

Circle of Life

A wolf pack must have one alpha, either a male or female, and usually contains an alpha pair with subordinate adult males or females, juveniles and pups. All individuals of the pack feed and care for the pups, protecting and teaching them the ways of the pack until age two when they enter the unit as equal members.

Only the alpha pair mates. Subordinate females do not come into heat, leaving the role of reproduction to the lead female. A young male often leaves the original group and becomes a disperser, roaming until he finds an unrelated pack to join, until he fights for an alpha spot in a rival pack, or until he finds a mate and establishes a new pack of his own.

Wolves don't name each other, but they do assign an identity to other pack members. They are smart, resourceful, and capable of deep emotion. They are loyal to each other and follow an established pack order. They mate for life.

Steady, an old she wolf lay under the snow-laden, low-hanging branches of a mature spruce. It was early spring and the cold and damp made the shoulder she'd damaged as a careless pup, tumbling off a rock ledge onto the ragged edge of a fallen log, hurt more than usual. Beside her lay Speed, her wise but failing, grizzled old mate.

If she were prey instead of an apex predator, the others would hunt the tracks and scent she left in the snow in their pursuit of game. Her uneven gait, heavier on her uninjured side, would tell them she might be vulnerable to attack. The frailties of old age betrayed her in the scent she left behind. Each season saw her lamer than the one before. It was only the existence and mercy of the pack that made her less vulnerable than a solitary, old, lame moose.

She had no way to count the number of years passing since she had first tottered out of the birth den with a sister and brother, but her bones and recollection told her it had been a long time. Her puppy year of play and even her early hunts had whizzed by as she remained with her pack when her brother left, erasing her memory of him.

Devoted to her alpha parents she had never mated or even come into heat, until her dam had been killed in a hunting accident. Looking for an unrelated bitch to take as a new mate, her sire had challenged Speed, the young male leader of a neighboring band, and had lost his sight and then his life to ensuing injuries. Speed's young mate had then attacked Steady who had come into heat after her mother's death, seeing this interloper as a competitor for dominance of the new, combined pack. Steady won the battle, killed her attacker and took her place as Speed's mate.

She had whelped only one litter in seven years, not an illustrious breeding career, but those years had seen drought come to the land. Game had grown scarcer with each passing season. The pack had ranged ever wider and wider in search of sufficient food as Speed and Steady's litter grew to adulthood.

Challenging other packs for hunting territory they had won and lost, at times widening their range and at other times losing a pack member to resulting injury or disease. Their largest daughter, Silver Haze, had joined one of those packs and then found her way back to her mother's side with three scorched pups in tow after having become separated from her mate while fleeing fire.

It was Haze who had given Steady grandchildren and Haze who was due to whelp again, lying in a den dug into an outcropping of rock. Old, grizzled Steady lay atop the outcropping next to the failing Speed. The new alpha of the pack, a large, lean, black, rangy four-year-old known as Night, lay outside the mouth of the den overlooking the members of his pack lounging in the snow below him.

  Night did not overtly watch the failing pair but was very much aware of the old she-wolf and her injured frame. The old patriarch had always been Speed to his mate's Steady, perceived as a strong, confident and fast-like-the-wind male with the female running steady at his side, matching him stride for stride, guarding his flank.

  Night's pack had been providing for the pair, respectful of their history and relationship to his mate. But, he had a litter of new mouths about to be born. Would he be able to provide for them all if the old pair could no longer hunt?

  As a past leader herself, Steady knew she and her mate were a liability to the pack. Though she lay still to not disturb Speed's fitful sleep, it seemed that her breathing alone caused him pain. He moaned weakly, almost imperceptibly, a sound so small that any but the closest of ears might have missed it.

  He coughed and a thick, foul smelling substance was loosened from his lungs and dribbled from his slack, greyed muzzle. She lifted her head from where it lay lightly against his shoulder and licked away the yellow ooze as it appeared.

  Steady had cared for Speed in this manner all night and into the morning without disturbing him. This time, however, he woke upon feeling her loving caress. Lifting his head, silvered fur whitened with a soft blanket of wet, spring snow, he turned pain and hunger dulled eyes towards hers. Struggling to breathe he held her gaze, saying good-by.

She had grown gaunt and weakened from the reduced rations she forced upon herself, sharing her part of the kill with him. Instinctively, she cared for him, always hoping that he, who had shared every day she could remember, would recover and run to hunt at her side once more. And, now his pain-filled eyes were saying good-by.

The effort of raising his head to look at her was too much for Speed and he collapsed in a fit of coughing. Night turned to regard the suffering old male unemotionally. Steady's other daughter, recognized as Smaller for her diminutive size and shy demeanor, jumped up from where she lay with the now two-year-pups from Haze's previous litter, and ambled over to where her parents lay.

Not wanting to be left alone, the gangly group of bored youngsters trotted behind her. Smaller approached the old pair slowly, head lowered, still respectfully of the previous status each wolf had held in her life. With eyes downcast to the snow and pine needle-covered ground, she tilted her head sideways offering her vulnerable throat to her mother.

As Steady weakly raised her greyed and thinning muzzle, welcoming her daughter's approach, Smaller lowered hers and rubbed it lovingly against her mother's neck. She dared not touch her father lest Steady change her mind and attack her seeing her approach or of the gang of youngsters behind her as a threat to the old male.

The emaciated bodies, weak movements and lusterless coats of both her parents coupled with the odors issuing from her listless sire told her she would soon be losing these two that had raised and eternally guided her. Looking over to where Night lay, she searched her new alpha's posture and demeanor for censorship of her next, intended action. Seeing none, she lay down in the snow and curled into a ball, bringing her tail up over her nose for warmth in a position that would put her as close to her parents as she could be without touching them.

It surprised her that two of Haze's pups lay down near her, curling into identical balls, willing to wait until she chose to get up and play with them again. The third pup trotted off with a pine cone in his mouth looking for a new playmate.

Steady closed her eyes and sighed peacefully. She had hunted with Speed in the fall when the kick of the cow elk they chased had injured him. Making the killing blow by ripping the juggler vein of the injured cow had given her little satisfaction when she saw Speed lying in blood saturated dirt with red froth bubbling from his slack muzzle.

She had lain with him all that afternoon while the others fed on the cow. Smaller had brought her parents a haunch and Steady had chewed and regurgitated meat for Speed, eventually enticing him to eat a small amount. After several hours, his condition had stabilized and she breathed easier thinking he would recover.

She had smelled the young, lone, disperser male at the same time Speed did. Even in his weakened condition, the old alpha recognized the challenge of a lone male approaching his pack and growled deep in his throat. As the black Night appeared at the edge of the clearing, Haze and Smaller had joined Steady to stand between the interloper and their downed sire. With teeth bared and hackles raised all three females snarled menacingly, willing to fight this new threat to the death if necessary, to protect the old male each knew could no longer protect himself.

Speed's females would make no challenge to the young male over alpha rights, but they would give the old patriarch the respect he was due. Accepting the situation for what was, Night simply walked confidently into the clearing and began to leisurely feed on the remains of the cow elk.

First Haze and then Smaller approached the newcomer with head lowered and tail tucked, welcoming him as a now much needed member of the pack. Steady stayed with her mate but made no further challenge to the pack's new leader. Within a month, Haze had come into heat and mated with Night, and thus the pair became the new alphas of the pack.

The old patriarch worsened over the winter months. Cold put sickness into his lungs and he fevered and wheezed. Finally, dehydrated and too weak to move with the pack, he lay down under the old spruce near the den where his daughter lay in labor.

As Speed closed his eyes for the last time, Steady lay her head against the neck of he who she had always loved. She heard the small whine of newborn pups. With a great shudder, Speed convulsed into what looked like smile at the sound and took his final breath.

Smaller whined. She wanted to push her muzzle against him and make him get up but her mother's expression told her to let him go. Steady licked her daughter's muzzle, sighed deeply and then lowered her head to once more lay against her mate's shoulder. Her family was safe. It was time to go with Speed. Closing her eyes, she waited for the wind to also carry her last breath away.

Heather Brenner is currently 35 years old. She resides in Cadillac, Michigan in a two bedroom apartment. As a very young child, she was diagnosed with a moderate case of Autism (a learning disability that impairs the brain).

On June 15, 1012, Heather lost her dad, Clarence Brenner at 66 years old due to heart trouble. Her mother, Patsy, currently at 70 years old still lives along with Heather's siblings, Lori and Allen. She has one nephew, Zach. She also has three nieces, Chelsea, Gabby and Tina, along with a great nephew, "Fate" William.

Blackjack-Roo is her pure black male cat who resides with her and provides lots of entertainment.

She is currently in a steady relationship with her boyfriend, Joel.

Heather graduated from Marion High School in Marion, Michigan in 2002. She was an active college student at Cadillac Baker College in Cadillac, Michigan from 2002-2006 and wasn't able to graduate since she couldn't finish all her schooling due to her disability.

Some of Heather's favorite hobbies and interests are: making homemade jewelry, writing poems and volunteer work at the Shepherd's Table twice every week on Tuesdays and Thursdays when needed.

Special Olympics 2017

It just seems like forever, for any given day, way back since in the early summer of 2012, that I, Heather Brenner, has really wanted to be an athlete for the Area 32 Special Olympics. During that time I still lived by myself in my old one bedroom home at Harbor View Apartments located near the 'Family Fare' Supermarket in Cadillac, Michigan.

The former apartment complex's service coordinator, Jennifer (aka Jenni) Johnson had assisted me to get all set up with them over time, as she then handed me over an application to complete for Area 32.

A day or so later my mother, Patsy Brenner, took me down to see my family physician at Tustin Family Practice in Tustin, Michigan (which is through the Spectrum Health Hospital in Reed City, Michigan) in order to have my physical completed before I could participate in the area 32 Special Olympics. Just shortly after my doctor completed the physical, she stated that I was up to date with all of my shots, including the tetanus shot, which I could believe is due every ten years. I was already set to head back for home.

After both my mother and I returned back to Harbor View I've simply handed in the completed application form back to Jenni Johnson, asking her on where it would be sent out to. She then helped me mail off the completed physical form and, in no time at all, that I was finally able to take part in any of the sporting events that I liked from that day forward.

However, at that time, I wasn't at all sure if I would have to find a way of my own transportation to any of the athletic events. Just recently, as of April 2017 my boyfriend, Joel, then told me how to get around by using the Tri-county Area busses. So I finally then decided to really give the Special Olympics a try this time.

So, as of late spring-early summer of 2017, it was my very first time doing my very best to attend every day of practice as I possibly could every Saturday, from 10:00 am until 12:00 pm. I have enjoyed every simple moment we were having at our practices each week at the Cadillac High School football stadium, off the corner of Chestnut and Linden Streets.

Other than practicing and working very hard for our track and field meets, it was also a fun and exciting experience for me, Joel and our fellow team mates. We had to do some of the exercises and stretching moves in between practices every Saturday.

One of the so-called crazy exercises that we all had to do was walking around on part of the track course back and forth, like ducks, and not quacking like them during that time! At first I was thinking to myself (so no one else hears me, not even Joel) about what I was really wanting to say about this exercise. I thought to myself, "How embarrassing could this get?" I asked myself a few times, but by the time I completed at lease five days of practice at the high school's track field, I was finally able to participate in my very first home meet-obviously held at the Cadillac High School.

Actually it was the very last and final home track meet of the year. So I was able to take advantage of the opportunity and won quite a few ribbons. I also had an amazing time with Joel and our fellow teammates at the good old Area 32 Special Olympics.

I've participated as much as I could this past year with the three track and field events as follows: 100 yard dash, 50 yard dash, and the softball throw. I remember the colors of the ribbons very well that day. The four colors are as follows: Blue is 1st place, Red is 2nd place, Yellow is 3rd place, and Green is for being a participant at 4th place and lower.

I've earned 2nd place running in the 100 yard dash, 3rd place running in the 50 yard dash, and a participant ribbon at 4th place in the softball competition. After all of the events came to an end, we celebrated our victories with light lunches to enjoy. They consisted of grilled hot dogs, potato chips, chocolate chip cookies and small cups of lemonade. The lunches, or course, were free of charge to all athletes, coaches and volunteers. Everyone else had to pay a small fee of $2.00 each.
    Everyone was there including my mother, Patsy Brenner, and our good loyal friend, Chrissy. Once I'd met up with my mother to sit down and eat with her, Joel walked up to us and asked me if I was going to the summer games event down in Mount Pleasant, Michigan for the first three day weekend of June. Laughing, I told him, "Well Sweetie pie, I'm just so excited for all of us to go because that was my plan originally! But, yes, I would really love to go!"
    He replied, "Okay Dear, I'm really hoping you get to be there with us."
    Then he took a bite of my hot dog sandwich as he walked off.
    As we have finished our final day of practice I asked about the summer games. One of the coaches informed me that I was short by just a few days of practice and I wasn't able to attend. At first I was really heartbroken in a way, and I didn't know how I would tell the others, especially Joel. I finally had to tell them everything. I've simply explained that I couldn't even ride with them on the bus until next year's season when I could attend enough days of practice first.
    I'm willing to win more ribbons and hoping that someday I'll receive a ribbon or so for 1st place! Hopefully next year I'll be able to go down to Mount Pleasant with Joel and the rest of the area 32 Special Olympics

gang for the summer games. I can hardly wait for that time to finally arrive.

I know deep within my heart I'll have such an amazing time being active with the summer games. There will always be many events and actives galore.

I'm hoping everyone in my immediate family will be there to cheer us on, plus a few close friends of both me and Joel's as well for more special needs adults to participate in their sporting events. As a matter of fact, I have so far encouraged at least two very close friends of Joel and I's without any hesitation. I'm hoping that someday soon they'll be fellow athletes in the Area 32 Special Olympics family!

Those two very close friends I speak of are Chrissy and John. We're hoping to find some more nominees out there living in Area 32's range. Chrissy wants to give the Special Olympics another try and if John went too at least, learn more on what the Special Olympics is all about.

Well, quite frankly I'm writing on that subject now. Everyone from the "Write to Publish" writer's group wanted me to write about my experiences with the Special Needs Adult Sporting Events. As a matter of fact, John is one of those from our writing group that really wanted me to submit something about this topic to begin with.

So I'm gladly taking this opportunity to do that, in fact, "no one-and I mean no one-is messing with a dummy here!" I'm not joking around either. I'm very serious about my commitment to do my best to improve both my writing and publishing, as well as my motor skills. It's just like how I feel about working at both my crafting projects and being very hard at working with my dish washing job. I take my writing skills seriously and I'm always playing hard in between so I can be in the very best shape I can be in my mind, body and in my spirit deep within my heart!

Betty L. Dowell

Betty Dowell was part of a large family of outcasts in a small town. She had ten siblings. After her father passed her mother married a man who added eight more children to the family. That made eighteen siblings. She was given to her grandmother at the age of seven. Her father passed away when she was nine.

Her grandmother had her telling made up stories to her siblings and cousins. That was her springboard to writing. She worked hard on the farm. Betty hoed fields, picked berries, waited tables, and baby sat to gain funds for college. Her degrees were a Bachelor of Science with an interdepartmental major of Computer Science and Mathematics. Her minor was in Accounting. She then earned a Masters in Computer Science. That activity kept the children out of mischief.

She married and had five babies plus five miscarriages. Her blood type was O- C- D-. Her husband had O + C + D+. That blood combination predicted fifty % miscarriages.

She now has five books published and is working on four which should be published before the year is over.

The Plucky Journey of Stacy

Stacy slowly became aware of the sun shining through the window onto her bed. She opened her grayish blue eyes. They had small hazel specs mixed into her eye. She climbed out of bed and excitedly dressed. She and her dad were going on a week long vacation to visit the Detroit Zoo and stay in a campground nearby. Her mother had passed on during the former month from cancer. Her dad was very depressed.

Stacy ran down the stairs barely able to contain her excitement. They had packed the car the night before. Her dad was standing at the table with breakfast set out. It consisted of pancakes, bacon, eggs, milk, and orange juice.

They were finally sitting in the front seat of the green Tempest. Stacy's dad was very tall and slender with blue eyes and a dark butch haircut. His name was Mack.

"Stacy, we're going to take the back roads. We're in no hurry, we have all week. Might as well do some sight seeing while we're at it," stated Mack.

"That sounds like fun dad," responded Stacy.

A few hours later, they were crossing a country bridge. It was narrow with metal sides and a top. A truck was approaching from the other side. As it crossed the bridge it blew a tire. It spun out of control and ran into the Tempest, crushing it against the rail. Mack ended up wedged between the steering wheel and the seat, unconscious. Stacie was thrown clear of the car and landed below in a very dense thicket that was on the bank of the river. She was also unconscious. When the rescuers arrived, they determined that Mack was in a coma. They had no idea that Stacy was on the river bank below.

It was dark when she regained consciousness. She looked up at the bridge and saw the Tempest was gone. She couldn't see her dad. Panicking, she called loudly for him. He didn't respond. She began to cry and climbed up onto the bridge. She sat on the edge for an hour before she decided that he wasn't coming back for her.

So what was she going to do? She decided to walk in the direction that they had been traveling. Even if she found a payphone, she didn't have money to pay for one. He wouldn't be home to answer the phone anyway.

Stacy walked down the road in the dark for a half hour or so. She was getting so tired and hungry, and hurt all over. Her legs and arms had deep cuts from being thrown into the brush. Curling up in the grass beside the road she went to sleep not realizing that she had lain down in poison ivy.

Soon the sun rose and Stacy woke up and continued walking on the road. She had no idea where it led; she only knew she was following the line that her dad had been on. It was around noon and she began itching all over and a rash appeared on her skin. She was so hungry when she spotted a garden patch. She collected tomatoes and pickles. She couldn't carry enough to last very long, so she devoured the food and then collected more.

Evening approached and she saw a gas station ahead. She hung around the station. Soon a car pulled in with one man in it. The car was traveling in the direction that she was. While the man was inside the station, she slipped into the car and slouched down on the floor behind the driver seat. The man happened to see her do it. He didn't acknowledge her presence and drove down the road. Soon he turned onto a trail into state land, then turned into the woods. Soon he pulled off the trail and got out, opened the back door and grabbed her arm. Recklessly he pulled her out onto the grass. It was obvious that he was drunk.

"My, my what a tasty little morsel you are, my child," he grunted as he unzipped his pants. He was drunk enough that his dropped pant legs caused him to stumble. Stacy took the opportunity to slip between his legs and run into the woods to hide. She watched from the bushes as the man floundered around. He finally got in his car and drove back out to the road. She remained hidden for about an hour and then ventured out onto the trail. She now had an extra mile to walk. Her body hurt from poison ivy, cuts, bruises, and hunger.

It was well into the afternoon when Stacy was standing outside of a cemetery. She now could add sunburn to her miseries. She recalled once during a camping trip, her dad had spread mud on her to keep her from getting sunburned. The cemetery where her mother was buried had water pumps in it. Perhaps this one did also. Stacy entered the gate and searched until she found a pump at the back. Pumping water onto the ground she created mud and coated herself. She covered her face, neck, ams, and legs. The cool mud felt very soothing. After it dried, it felt itchy and drew her skin taut. Insects didn't seem to bite through the dried mud either. It wasn't long and she was approaching a small town. She found a park that had bathrooms.

She went in and washed up. She wanted to be presentable if she was seen by the town inhabitants. She was still hungry.

She went into the alley behind a restaurant. She planned to sit and wait for the staff to throw away fresh food. Finally a man wearing a cook's apron threw something in the garbage can. In the meantime a pit bull also descended on the can. He took a defensive stance between Stacy and the can and showed his teeth as he growled at her. She backed up and watched him eat until he had eaten his fill and lay down. Stacy warily approached the can while talking to the dog, as she hoped to gain his trust. She did and he pranced up to her with his tail wagging. After Stacy had her fill, she walked out onto the sidewalk in the front. To her amazement the pit bull followed her. He was now her companion, which gave her a sense of safety.

It started to rain. She looked around and saw a school in the next block. Running to it she stood under the overhang of the door. She noticed a railroad behind the school. Trying to stay under the eaves, she went to the back. Once in back, Stacy saw a train setting on the track. She ran to the station and told the man that her mother had sent her to find out where the train was going.

"Detroit," was the answer.

It was time for her to retreat for a little distance. Then she snuck back to the train. She and her new dog slipped into a box car. This train was going to take her where she wanted to go.

There were two men in the car.

"Well, looky here. Clean this little muppet up and she would bring a pretty chunk of money in the black market."

They began to surround her when the pit bull drove them out of the boxcar. There was a calico cat in the car who hissed and snarled at the two of them. There was no place for it to go. Slowly Stacy and the pit bull got its trust. I think I will call you Callie," she said to the cat, "as for you dog, I will call you Pal."

The Mighty Smudge

This story is about a female dog with unbelievable heart. I will begin with the male that sired her. He, himself, was a very gifted dog. He adopted the family. This furry little ball of energy came through a hole in the fence. He belonged to a family that lived behind them. The puppy attached himself to the son. He appeared right when it was time for Carole to pick her husband up from work. She told her son, "You cannot have that pup. You take it around the block and tell them their pup came to us through the fence."

Sam reluctantly walked off with the puppy with tears in his eyes. Soon he came back. "Mom, their dog has a litter of puppies. The lady said I could keep this one!"

Carole loaded the kids in the car. The puppy tried to get in the car too, but Carole took it back to the porch commanding, "You STAY here!"

She got into the car and backed out of the driveway. They lived on a four lane intersection. The puppy ran after the car barking.

Carole assured the kids, "He will go back, because he can't keep up with the car."

She looked in her rear view mirror and the puppy was running after them amidst four lanes of cars. "Oh my goodness, he is going to get hit. I'll just have to take him into the car."

Carole pulled into the next parking lot to try to retrieve the him. He made it safely to her. "If that pup wants to be with us that badly, we will keep him," she stated.

The puppy settled into the family very well. Sam decided to call him Smoky. He was a mixed breed, but had the black and brown markings of a German Shepherd. The dog was highly intelligent. Not only did he learn tricks quickly, he made up some of his own. Although he was friendly and loved people, he was protective of the children and Carole.

On one occasion Carole's husband, John, was wrestling with her on the floor. Smoky grabbed his arm and even drew a little blood. Another time John's brother was babysitting and grabbed one of the boys. Smoky had him down in a flash. After that when he wanted to play with one of the kids, John's brother put the dog out.

A strange thing did occur once when Carole was after the kids. John's dad was standing watching and commented, "Well why didn't Smoky get after you?"

Carole looked up at the dog. He was slinking off with his head down and his tail between his legs. "I don't know," she answered.

One day Smoky came up missing. The kids walked the neighborhood calling for him. John and Carole drove around town looking for him. He was nowhere to be found. Days passed. They went to the animal shelter to see if he was there. He was not. The kids cried often because they missed him. The family resigned themselves to the conclusion that he was truly gone.

A few months passed and Sam came running into the house, "Smoky is back!"

The family ran to the window and watched him coming down the sidewalk. They opened the door and he walked through it like he had been there all the time. Carole noticed a new tag on his collar. "What do you have here boy?"

The tag had the name Irving stamped on it with a phone number. They called Smoky using the strange name on the tag and he responded. Carole called the number, "Are you missing a dog named Irving?"

The woman's voice on the other end sounded very excited, "Yes. I was so worried about him."

"Well, he came home," Carole replied. "We've been

searching for him. I have little kids that cried a lot be cause they had lost their dog. His name is actually Smoky."

"Oh my, we are an elderly couple and will miss him. I wouldn't want to take him away from little children. You keep him."

Carole thanked her graciously. After that they kept testing the dog. He responded to either name. Time passed and the family relocated. They moved into a house that sat far off the road, in the middle of the woods. No one could tell that anyone lived back there. Smoky loved his new environment. He hunted, went swimming and just plain enjoyed life. He sill kept an ever watchful eye on the family.

United Parcel Service delivered a package one day. The dog was nowhere to be seen. The oldest girl came out into the yard to receive the package. Suddenly Smoky appeared and had the delivery man's arm in his mouth. The man was handing a clip board to the girl for a signature. She started to reprimanded the dog.

"Oh, he's ok. He didn't actually bite me; he just wanted to prevent me from touching you."

On another occasion, a possum was at the back door. The children opened the door to see what the noise was. Without hesitation, Smoky forced his way past them through the door and killed the possum in seconds. They started poking at the dead possum. Smoky growled at the kids and killed the possum again. This little endeavor was repeated a few times. Finally Smoky killed it again and carried the possum off into the woods where the kids couldn't find it.

He obeyed commands to a fault. Sarah, the oldest, went to visit the neighbors and took Smoky with her. She walked down the drive and ordered him to stay at the entrance. They had dogs and she didn't want them to get into a fight. Some time had passed and Sarah went home out the back door and though the woods. She forgot that Smoky was at the neighbors drive entrance. John came home from work and was not met by the dog.

"Where is Smoky?" he asked, as he entered the house. "He usually meets the car when I pull in the driveway. He didn't do that tonight."

"I don't know," Carole answered.

All of a sudden Sarah jumped up. "I told him to stay at the neighbors drive. I forgot him and came home the back way!"

The family all went running out to the road. They could see smoky patiently waiting down the road at the driveway. He had been waiting for several hours.

John and Carole bought half carcasses at the butchers for their meat. When John picked up the packaged meat, he always had Smoky with him. John took a box out and placed it in the station wagon, right next to Smokey. When he went back in to get the next package the butcher was waiting for him. "Aren't you afraid that dog will get into your meat?"

"No, he won't touch it."

So the butcher asked John to wait a few minutes. They stood inside watching the dog through the window. Smoky made no move towards the meat. "That is some dog! I am going to give you a bone for him."

After that Smoky got a meat covered leg bone every time John made trips to the butcher.

One day John came home to find the kids and Smoky not home. "Where are the kids?" he asked Carole.

"They went into the woods."

"How long ago was that?"

"It's been a few hours."

"I'm going to call them."

"Why are you worried? They know the woods as they

have Smoky. He will take care of them."

John went to the edge of the woods and called the children. After several minutes they still had not answered him. He went to the car and honked the horn several times. When he didn't get a response, he drove around the mile. He kept stopping to call and honk the horn. He kept increasing the area of search. Finally he saw the group coming out of the woods three miles from the house. They had gotten lost and Smoky had led them out of the woods to the road.

John had a thoroughbred beagle. She gave birth to a litter of puppies that were a mix of Smoky and the beagle. One little female was a mirror image of him. The kids decided to call her Smudge for little Smoky. She was the most venturesome and intelligent pup of the litter. John found it impossible to kennel her. First she dug out from under the fence. So John buried a wall underneath the fence level. The day he installed the wall he put the puppies inside the fence. Smudge beat him to the house.

He put her back inside the fence and watched her. She held her back to the dog coop and placed her feet on the fence, then shinned herself upward till she could get over the fence. He placed a piece of fence that slanted inward all around the fence top. She beat him to the house again. He watched to see how she did it. She climbed on top of the coop from the front and jumped over the fence. That was the end of John's endeavors to pen up the puppies.

The neighbors had a very large black german shepherd. He came visiting often. One day he arrived just as Carole had fed the puppies. The shepherd started sniffing their food. Smudge set all our paws in a firm stance and snarled at the dog. He was at least four times her size. Carole grabbed smudge up exclaiming, "You're biting off more than you can chew, you silly pup!"

A year passed and Smoky disappeared. John drove

around looking for him while the kids searched the woods. Two days went by and there was no sign of him. On the third day Carole went to the garden. She noticed something out of place in the weeds at the ditch. Upon investigating, she discovered Smoky lying in the tall grass. She carried him into the house where John examined the dog.

"Somebody shot him with a shotgun. We need to get him to the vet. Apparently it took him three days to make it home."

John put Smoky in the staton wagon. The family headed for the veterinarian, which was several miles away. Upon reaching the office, he carried Smoky inside. "Our dog's been shot. He was missing for days before he made it home."

The vet placed him on a table and shaved what appeared to be the injured area. Once the hair was removed, you could see holes all over his body. "I just can't understand anyone purposelessly shooting a family pet. Did he run deer?"

"No. If he did I would understand him being shot."

"I would put him to sleep, but I am reluctant to do so. He has fought this hard to stay alive. I'll give him a pain killer and you take him home. Let's give him a chance to fight this."

When they got Smoky home, they put him on the bed. One or more of the family members sat on the bed with their hand reassuringly on the dog. He would open his eyes from time to time and look at them, and then give half a tail wag and close his eyes again. He finally passed away at three **in** the morning. The family held a tearful burial at the edge of the woods.

In the meantime Smudge was getting more mature. She went missing. Carole heard a dog barking off in the woods. There were wild dog packs in the area and Carole thought the barking was from them.

In a couple of days, a neighbor pulled in the drive. He asked Carole to come to his car and identify a dog. It was Smudge. "I found her in the woods behind the house. She had her back leg wrapped up in wire fence."

There was a line on Smudge's leg. The skin was severed apart all the way around the leg. Carole carried her to the station wagon. John was out of town on a job and couldn't help. She drove over to her father-in-laws house. "Dad, come to the car and look at Smudge," she said.

When he saw the dog, he replied, "If it were my dog, I would put her down. It would be the compassionate thing to do."

Carole got very agitated, "If you broke your leg, should I just shoot you?"

He laughed his whisky laugh and watched her back the car out onto the road. When Carole got the dog home, she wrapped the leg in a bandage laced with bag balm. A few days passed with Carole keeping the wound dressed. The flesh on the leg was shrinking until there was about a half inch between the two sections. Carole quit dressing it. Smudge ran on three legs. The wounded leg would swing in the air and make a creaking sound. It began to smell very rank and the lower leg turned black.

Carole decided that the leg had to come off. She didn't have enough money to go to the vet so decided the she would have to cut the leg off herself. She knew how to cut off the leg of a chicken and decided to use the same method. She was worried that it would hurt the dog. Smudge gave no reaction at all while Carole worked on her.

The upper leg sealed over well. Smudge could run as fast as any of the other dogs on her three legs. She even caught rabbits.

Then one day the family came home and found her lying on the front steps dead. Someone had shot her too.

John A. Filley was born on December 06, 1983. He lives in Cadillac, Michigan in an apartment on Lake Cadillac. He graduated from Marion High School in 2002, and attended Baker College in 2003 and 2004.

John has two older brothers. His parents were both teachers, and are now retired.

He belongs to a writers group called Write to Publish. The following are his first stories to be published. John started writing in 2004 but never tried to publish any early works.

His interests are horror, suspense, sci-fi, fantasy, comedy, thriller, and mystery stories. Writing gives John a sense of self-worth and creativity. He is still learning this craft. Write to Publish has helped him to develop his talent and skill.

John A. Filley

I'll Own You Then Kill You

   Why hello there, I bet you're wondering who or what I am, but I'll save that part for last. I'll start first by how most people acquire me. Usually you receive me from a stranger for free. After you use me you'll be hooked and start paying money to have more of me. After spending all your income you'll still want more, and spend your entire savings for college to get more of me. But even this won't be enough and you'll still crave more. It won't matter how much you have, you'll always want more.
   I'll wreck your home, rip apart your family, take your children away, and that's just how I'll begin. The sadness I bring is a sight to see even though I cost more than gold and more than diamonds, it won't matter because you'll still want more of me. Rich or poor, black or white, Christian or atheist, your status doesn't matter to me. I'll make you commit crimes and the worst of all sins, using me will make you feel possessed by an unworldly and ungodly power. I'll make you lie to your father, steal from your mother, and cause bad injuries to your sisters and brothers. The things that you do should make you feel bad, but you won't since I numb any pain and thinking ability you would have had. Eventually they'll have enough and kick you out of your home.
   I'll make you forget how you were raised and forget all your morals. I'll be your conscience and you'll do as I say. Your looks and your pride, you'll lose both of those too. You may have even had a chance in the future to be president. In the future you may have had a beautiful spouse, a great family, millions in cash, huge house, and awesome career, but the chances of them are gone now since you chose me over them. I'll take and I'll take until you have nothing left to give.
   The things I'll do to you, you won't know reality. I'll

remove all of your sanity. I'll make you see visions, and make you hear voices. You won't sleep very much because I'll keep you up at night, and when you do sleep, the nightmares I cause will ensure it won't be for long. I'll make you cry, laugh, sweat, shake and hallucinate. But by now its too late, you're under my control. The more you use me the more I won't let go and in a short time I will own your mind, body, and soul.

  I sound like the worst friend in the world and you're right, I am. But you don't care, you still won't stop using me. That day with the stranger you could have said no and walked away then. But you didn't, and now we're inseparable. I'll even be with you deep down in your grave.

  It sounds like Frodo and the ring doesn't it? The ring constantly ruining the owner's body and mind until the ring is the only thing the owner has left. But *Lord of the Rings* is entirely fiction and unlike that, I'm totally real. You probably still wonder what I am by now, and if you haven't guessed, most people call me drugs.

Always Half Awake

Cops and a detective were outside the bar where a man had just killed another man. In a drunken brawl he killed him with a broken bottle. They had the whole area cordoned off and a few groups of on-lookers stood on the outside of it spectating the scene.

A couple cops asked him, "Why did you kill the guy? How did you kill the guy? Was it a spur of the moment? Did you know who he was before you fought with him?"

But the murderer just sat on the bench, handcuffed, not answering either of them, in fact not even responding. Eventually two officers took each of his biceps and walked him to a police car, placing him in the back seat. They took him to a police station where they booked him and put him in a jail cell for the rest of the night. (The whole night he just sat upright on the edge of his bed never sleeping and never saying a single word to anyone).

The next day the detective, a criminal psychologist, the district attorney, and his lawyer all asked him: "Why did you kill the man in the bar?"

The man was more talkative today than the night before when he was arrested. He kept replying to each of them, "I didn't kill anyone and I don't know anything about any murder. I don't even know why you're keeping me in jail. If someone was murdered, I had nothing to do with it."

They returned him to his jail cell where he laid on his back gazing at the wall. After an hour he sat upright on the edge of the bed for the entire night, still not sleeping.

The next day the detective and criminal psychologist questioned him again. They determined he didn't really fit the profile for a criminal. He kept denying everything they were accusing him of. If he was lying about not re membering and not believing he was involved, he didn't act like he was lying. Sociopaths are usually great liars and great criminals, but they determined he wasn't a sociopath either. He also didn't fit the profile for someone having schizophrenia or a multiple personality disorder.

They returned him to his jail cell for the night. Again he just sat on the edge of the bed, not saying anything to anyone and not sleeping either.

The next day the criminal psychologist asked him: "When do you sleep?"

The man replied, "What are you talking about? I go to sleep most nights at about 7 pm. I know it may sound weird to sleep 12 hours a night, but I wake up most mornings about 7 am.

The criminal psychologist said: "No, the guards say they see you sitting on the edge of your bed all night with your legs dangling over the sides. You must be awake, not sleeping. So, when do you sleep? Most people can't go more than three days without sleep, even extreme insomniacs manage to get to sleep on the third night."

The man just shook his head and denied the criminal psychologist's claim that he never slept. The criminal psychologist and detective both noted that at no point did the man ever show signs of sleep withdrawal, though he did blink twice as much as the average person. The man was returned his cell and once again he never slept the whole night.

The next day the criminal psychologist called his old university professor, who taught at a university in a neighboring state. The professor agreed to pay a visit to the jail with some special machines he had.

When the professor came, they applied electrodes to various parts of the man's scalp. When they looked at the monitor which displayed the heat signatures of the man's brain, they were surprised with what they saw. The left half of the man's brain showed the colors red and green, which are the normal colors for someone's brain when they're awake. But the right half showed the colors black and blue, which were the normal colors for when someone is asleep. At no time should the colors of someone's brain be different colors on the opposite sides, like the monitor was showing the man's brain to be.

The professor said, "The only known animal that has the ability for half its brain to sleep is the dolphin. This is how they manage to surface for air and not drown when sleeping. One half of its brain sleeps at a time. But what we're witnessing here should be impossible for a human to be able to do."

The professor and criminal psychologist spent the whole day and night running tests on the man. At the end they came to the conclusion that the man must have had a twin brother before he was born. Most of the time one twin envelopes the other twin at the beginning of pregnancy becoming something like an alpha male. Seldom are both twins born. Extremely rare are for both twins to be born merged to each other, like Siamese twins, which somewhat seemed to be this man's case. Even though Dr. Jekyll and Mr. Hyde is fiction, they decided what this man was going through was similar.

During the morning and afternoon the man was his usual self getting along with people, going to work and so on but during the evening and night he seemed to be someone entirely different being aggressive, obtuse, and more easily instigated. Unfortunately for the man, since he could not control himself at night, he spent the rest of his life in a sanitarium under the supervision of doctors and guards who constantly watched him.

Worse Than Hell

Jamal Barker woke up somewhere he didn't recognize. Everywhere he looked everything seemed to be on the verge of death. There were trees but they all had half of their leaves missing. The remaining leaves were brown and shriveling. There was grass, but none of it was bright green, it was all half green and half brown. He looked to his right and saw a river, but instead of it being the normal bluish-clear color it had somewhat of a brown color. To his left he saw a thin, pale chipmunk. It wasn't running away from him like he would've expected. He could see the chipmunk breathing and if it weren't for that he'd have guessed it was dead. The sun was barely visible behind a thin gray cloud cover that stretched across the entire sky.

Jamal got up off the ground and looked at the river next to him. Beside the river he saw a small wooden dock with a wooden boat tied to it. He walked onto the dock and saw a skeleton wearing a black cloak and with both hands on the oars. He believed it was a costume and the whole situation was some kind of a joke or prank.

He asked the person, "What's goin' on here?"

The person replied, "You died from a gunshot to the head during a gang shootout. This is the gateway to where you go next. Get on the boat, and I'll take you to where you belong."

Jamal said, "You stupid? I wanna know where this is and why I'm here! You better start making sense."

The person replied, "I can see that gun holstered in the back of your pants and know you're considering killing me if I don't give you the answers you want. Go ahead and kill me. What you"ll get is a punishment just as bad as hell, if not worse, while doing me a great favor. And I already told you where you are and why you're here, whether you believe it or not."

Jamal started to get his gun out to shoot the person, but reconsidered and walked away saying, "Forget you, dummy."

The person in the boat called after him, "You can leave and go wherever you want, but eventually you will come back here. Everybody comes back here in time."

Jamal walked in the opposite direction of the dock until the river was no longer visible behind him. It was then a fog engulfed him, it was so dense he couldn't see his own hand in front of him. Five minutes passed when suddenly the fog dissipated and he was back in his old neighborhood in the Bronx.

He went home to his family's apartment and found his mother clearing out his room and throwing his stuff away. He yelled at her to stop and tried to get her attention, but she seemed not to even notice he was there. He finally got mad enough he tried to slap her face, but she didn't even notice this, and he saw his hand pass right through her without feeling or hearing the hit.

Exasperated, he then went to his high school and saw most of his friends crying. He tried talking to them and received the same redaction his mother gave him. He skipped class, like he did half the time, and heard over the hallway speakers the principal announce his death and that counseling was available for anyone who wanted it.

He spent the night at home with everyone ignoring him. He didn't know where to be or where he wanted to go.

The next day he followed his mother outside heading wherever she was going. She walked to a funeral home half a mile away. Once there he saw many of his relatives and friends. Still everyone was giving him no reaction. He looked inside the coffin and saw himself. He realized that the person inside the boat was telling the truth. He really was dead.

He decided he wanted to go back to that place to talk to the person in the boat, but he had no idea how to get back there. He was quickly wrapped in the thick fog again and in five minutes he was back where everything was almost dead, but couldn't die.

He easily found the person still in the boat, still in costume, and still at the small dock. He went to the person to get more answers.

He asked the person, "Who a' you and what is this place?"

The person replied, "I am the Grim Reaper. Think of this place as the port to the afterlife. It's not earth, heaven, hell, or purgatory, but connected to all four. When someone dies they come here, and I take them to whatever afterlife they belong.

Jamal asked, "And where that? You gonna take me to hell, ain't you?"

The Grim Reaper replied, "I don't judge any of the people that I take to where they belong. I don't know where you're going, and I don't care. My job is to take the dead to where they belong, not to decide where they go."

Jamal thought back to the time when he was a gang member and the things he'd done. Selling drugs on the street, robbing a fast food restaurant at gun point, murdering an old man and his wife......The list of his evil actions went on and on. He was sure the Grim Reaper was going to row him to hell.

Jamal pulled out his gun and aimed it at the Grim Reaper's head saying, "Hear this skull face, I ain't gettin' on ya' boat, and I ain't goin' ta hell. I'll send you there before I let you take me there!"

The Grim Reaper replied, "When I said you'd be doing me a favor by killing me, I meant it. I've been doing this for well over a century. At no point has this job been fun for me, and the thought that I might be able to eventually go to hell myself is my only hope. I know hell won't be pleasant, but even burning there for eternity has to be better than this. So go ahead Jamal, if you really wanna kill me, then pull the trigger and blow a hole through my soul."

Jamal kept his handgun pointed at the Grim Reaper's head for a few more seconds, wondering what else he should ask the Grim Reaper before shooting him.

Jamal asked him, "Okay, say I do kill you what'll happen ta me? I just won't be able ta go ta hell, right? What else?"

"Yes, you will be unable to go to hell. You will also take my spot on this boat until someone like you comes to kill you. I was a Confederate soldier in the Civil War when I died, and much like you, I was dumb enough to kill who was the Grim Reaper at the time. I've been here ever since. If anyone does kill you, you will have the choice again to go to whichever afterlife you belong."

Jamal thought about it for a few more seconds before finally killing the Grim Reaper. There was flash of darkness for a second, and Jamal found himself in the boat where the Grim Reaper had been. His hands were wrapped around the oars of the boat. He couldn't take them off. He was stuck to the seat. He couldn't stand, as if his rear was nailed down. He looked up at the dock and saw a man, slightly older that him, in a Civil War Confederate Army soldier's uniform.

"Well, well. Look who it is. Thank you, sir, for murdering me, and you can call me Robert," the soldier said.

Jamal cried, "What this, you din't say it be like this!"

Robert replied, "Sure I did. You asked what would happen if you killed me and I said you would have to replace me, possibly for eternity. Unless you meant being unable to move, but you didn't ask about that."

"Really," Jamal asked, "I cant move at all?"

Robert climbed into the boat saying, "Nope, with the exception of rowing the oars back and forth, you really can't move at all."

As Jamal started rowing Robert to his afterlife, Robert said to him, "I thought I should tell you this, since you were nice enough to kill me: There are a few things you have to do as the Grim Reaper, and a few things you can't. Being unable to move is just the beginning. You can't lie; anything someone asks, you have to reply honestly, which includes why they don't want to kill you. Whoever dies and talks to you, you automatically know everything about them from their second of birth. Words really can't express, though, how grateful I am that you killed me. Having to take everyone to the afterlife after they died really hurt my heart, especially babies. Be it men who died of old age, stone cold serial killer gang members's like yourself, and even still born babies who never even had a chance to breathe, it was my job to take them all to the after life."

A blanket of white fog enveloped them for five minutes before they arrived at the shore of a beach with dark brown sand. The sky was dark gray and the sun wasn't visible. They didn't see living animals, but saw a carcass from a creature they couldn't identify.

"I've seen this place before and I think it's hell or just the beginning of it. Well, goodbye Jamal," Robert said, before he walked away.

Jamal actually did spend all of eternity as the Grim Reaper. Aside from not being able to move, he didn't dislike it as much as Robert did. Since he used to be a sociopathic gang member who killed people, taking dead babies to the afterlife was easier on him than anyone else.

Sherrie Fuscone was born near Indianapolis, Indiana, and moved to Chicago, Illinois as a baby. She grew up and stayed in the Chicago area until she retired to northern Michigan.

She began her professional life as a chemist in an industrial hygiene laboratory. Later, when she started a family, she went back to college and became a Registered Nurse, and practiced over thirty years in the Chicago area, then a short time in Michigan.

Sherrie is divorced and has raised two sons. Her older son and his family live in northern Illinois. She lost her younger son when he was twenty-two years old. Her only grandson is an eighteen year old high school senior. Her son and grandson also write.

There are two books for sale on **Amazon.com** and Kindle by Sherrie Ramsey Fuscone. One is about ghosts and the other is a novel for which Sherrie shares credit with her Aunt Thelma Ramsey, who didn't write, but who provided most of the research information.

Sherrie likes writing about history and science. She loves writing mysteries and humor. She has also written several children's books, as yet unpublished.

DAVID AND THE INJURED GOSLING

By Sherrie Fuscone

Meanings of Elfin Names:

Aelvara/Aelvar = of the elfin army

Aelfreda/Aelfred = an elfin counselor

Oberon = elfin ruler

Aelvara and Aelfreda Oberon were small, thin one-hundred-year-old twins who had been born with a full head of white hair and pointed ears. Aelvara (known as Alvie) and Aelfreda (known as Freda) had been named after twin uncles with similar slight but extremely strong bodies and the white elfin hair and pointed ears, too. The rest of the Oberon family looked like typical people. The elfin traits only came out in twins because each twin complemented the other in much of what they were born to do in the world. Twins always had a secret language of their own that only they could understand. Elfin twins had many secret ways that only they could share, especially in the making of potions. Their elfin ancestors lived very long lives and were always a force for good in the world.

Alvie and Freda were educated in Elfin magic by their uncles. Actually it was not magic at all, but only seemed like it to humans who, compared to elves, really had no clear understanding of the animals, the plants, and the earth itself. Their "magic" potions were simply made from the same animal, vegetable, and mineral ingredients found in all forests, plains, deserts, and mountainsides. The secrets were which of the ingredients they used together and the amount of each that was needed for particular uses. Over the centuries, the elfin families had made some of their magic known to humans when they thought they were ready. The elfin purpose in the world was to bring harmony and happiness to all the animals, plants, and humans who inhabited the places around them. The Oberon twins were only happy when they were doing good.

When their uncles died, Alvie and Freda inherited the huge heavily wooded Oberon estate. It was a place of good and evil to visitors, depending on what their intentions were. Bad-hearted people were afraid to enter the Oberon forest, but people with good hearts were especially favored visitors who often felt at perfect peace immediately upon entering the elfin woods.

The Oberon twins took a nice long nature walk every morning down a path in their woods known only to them. The sisters loved everyone but needed tranquility and a place to themselves so they would not be seen by humans.

As usual Alvie hurried ahead at a rapid pace down the path. She was the athletic one who liked plenty of exercise. She was very strong and exceptionally fast, but she never really paid attention to anything unless it was something she was seeking.

Freda on the other hand did not miss a thing in front, below, above, or on either side of her. She ambled along at a slower pace, preferring to exercise her mind instead. One morning she noticed something was out of place in the tall grass growing near the path. She stopped and bent down to inspect what at first appeared to be a dirty white tennis ball with moving legs. To her horror it was a gosling with its abdomen split open. Its mouth was agape and its eyes were closed in obvious pain as it kicked and tried to move its immature wings.

"Alvie, you can run faster than I. Please go get a box to make a bed for this gosling. It is horribly injured, but is still alive and suffering!"

"Oh, the poor little thing!" Alvie looked at the injured baby bird. "I'll hurry."

When Freda looked up, Alvie was gone.

From the supplies she carried in a small backpack, Freda put a temporary bandage on the gosling's abdomen. She poured a few drops of an instant pain-relieving potion from a small vial into the young bird's mouth. The gosling calmed down immediately and opened its eyes. When Alvie arrived with a shoe box Freda quickly made a bed of grass and moss for the gosling. Alvie then gently placed the young bird onto it, and put the lid over the top of the box to keep the baby goose warm as they hurried home. Once they were back home Alvie set the box with the injured bird down on the kitchen table. "Freda, you do the honors. You're more patient than I am with sewing," Alvie admitted.

Freda immediately opened a vial containing a yellow potion and put a few drops onto the bird's exposed internal organs. She then sewed up the torn muscles and skin with painstaking accuracy. During the entire procedure the injured gosling eyed her carefully, but it never once flinched or cried out in pain. Freda poured a few more drops of the yellow potion onto the stitches and covered the wound with a light dressing.

The next morning the gosling was moving around inside the box, making hungry noises. Freda took a peek at the baby bird and said, "Alvie, can you find the gosling's parents? It needs to go home now."

Alvie picked up the box with great care and disappeared quickly down the secret path. She returned a short time later and reported, "As per the rules, I had to give the baby bird back to whoever brought it to us. I had to give it back to a boy named David. He knew if he put the injured bird in our woods, we'd help it. It was David who took the gosling back to its parents."

Freda closed her eyes and described what she saw in the recent past, "In my mind's eye I see David tried to stop three older bully boys from hitting a bunch of helpless goslings with golf clubs. I see the bullies hit him, too, and chased him up a tree. They then returned and killed all the goslings except the one David brought to us. I see the Canadian geese crying in anguish when they found their dead babies."

Freda opened her eyes briefly and took a deep breath. She closed her eyes again and explained what she saw for the near future. "There will be more trouble for David from these older bullies. David is a worthwhile boy who must be protected, Alvie."

"I'll protect him and give him strength," Alvie stated with conviction. Then she added, "I also know how to punish and change the bullies, but it will take several months to make it permanent." Alvie then smiled to reassure her sister that harmony would return to their woods.

It was later that night when Alvie climbed a tree near David's house and entered his bedroom without a sound. She found a baseball bat on the floor next to a baseball tucked neatly in a catcher's mitt. She opened her backpack and took a small amount of earth from the Oberon's secret path and sprinkled it around these sports items. She thought to herself, *That should do the trick.*

As silent as a windless night, she slipped into the kitchen. In the refrigerator she found a big bottle of apple juice. *Perfect*, Alvie thought to herself. She giggled softly as she poured a few drops of a special pink elfin tonic into the bottle while thinking, *David and his whole family may be in for a few surprises.*

Alvie then moved like moonlight over the hills and entered the homes of each of the three bullies. On their foreheads she made a special elfin mark with a liquid from a tiny amber bottle, and she carried off all the golf clubs she found in their houses. She later buried these golf clubs at the exact spot where the injured gosling was found in their woods. Before going home, Alvie made a quick trip to the nearby lake to reassure the Canadian Geese and make them feel safer.

Soon it was time for baseball tryouts at the local middle school. David sat with his friends in the bleachers, waiting for his turn to demonstrate his skill at pitching, catching, and batting for the coaches. The three bullies sat down behind him after they had tried out but failed to be chosen for the team. They were angry and took out their irritation on David. They annoyed him with insults; pulled off his baseball cap; knocked down his bat and mitt; and "accidentally" kicked him in the back until it was his turn to try out.

In spite of the harassment David had an especially positive mental attitude that morning. He pitched and managed to strike out every batter standing in front of him. He ran fast and kept his eye on every ball batted to him in the field, which he caught without fail. When it was time to bat, David started out hitting to the infield, but his confidence grew with each pitch and was soon hitting the ball way over the high fence. His friends from school were shouting and whistling encouragement to him until the coach gave him the "thumbs up" sign. He was on the team!

All the kids went wild in the bleachers, yelling, clapping, and stomping their feet. All the kids were happy for David except the three bullies. They suddenly developed severe stomach pains, threw up, and had to go home to bed. In fact, from that day on, every time one of them was mean to anyone or anything, he developed terrible pains in his stomach and got sick. By the time school was out for the year, the three boys were a lot nicer and didn't bully anyone.

David continued playing baseball and was excellent at it. In fact his whole family was surprised at how each of them had become so much stronger, especially if they drank their apple juice. Dad and Mom could beat all their friends at doubles tennis. David's brother became the highest scoring forward on his soccer team. David's sister could do the most difficult vaults of anyone on her gymnastics team.

The best thing was the happiness of the Canadian geese because the Oberon sisters promised to prevent anybody from ever hurting their goslings again. When the geese finally flew south that Fall, the injured gosling had grown into a handsome gander and a strong flier that easily kept up with the rest of his flock.

"Well, what do you think, Sister?" Alvie asked Freda. "Do you think our uncles would be proud of how we kept the harmony in a complicated situation?"

Freda smiled in contentment, "Yes, I'm sure they would be.

Mrs. Chutney's Eulogy

Paul and Regina Rosini walked up to the casket to pay their respects. The deceased was a small thin woman with hair that was completely white and eyebrows that were still dark. Her face belied her true age of eighty-eight. She looked as if she were just resting her eyes and might sit up at any moment.

"My God, how I hated that old broad when I was a kid!" Paul said with feeling. He was a good-looking dark-eyed man of medium height. He was fit and trim with wide shoulders and his short dark hair sported a little gray at the temples.

"If you hated her so much, what are we doing here?" Regina turned her head in surprise. Regina was a pleasantly rounded brunette with dark hair and wide gray eyes in her pretty face. "I don't understand."

"No, I guess you wouldn't Honey." Paul looked at the old woman as if trying to memorize her face. Tears glistened in his eyes. "She's responsible for every success I have today. I'm older now and it was only when I heard she'd died that I realized how much I owed her."

Another couple walked up to pay their respects to the woman. The tall heavy-set man with salt and pepper hair put his hand on Paul's shoulder as if to comfort him. Paul turned to find an old friend from his school at his side.

"Vinnie! What are you doing here? I heard you moved to California and were some kind of bigwig in Silicon Valley. How did you hear about the old lady?" Paul quickly wiped at his eyes with his hand.

"Oh, I keep track of things. You do know my Ma still lives here in Newark? If anyone knows what's going on anywhere in this town, it's Ma." Vincent Addario smiled at his old Friend. "I heard you'd gone off to war, but I never knew what happened to you after that. You aren't still living in Newark or Ma would've told me."

"No. I'm currently stationed in Washington, D.C. I saw my share of action, but managed to get out in one piece. I was promoted to sergeant in the field, but left for a while to go to college on the V.A. plan. I went to Officer's Training School when I re-enlisted. I'm now a full colonel. Actually my wife and I have lived all over the world," Paul explained. "We just came back for Mrs. Chutney's funeral."

"Wow, I feel as if I ought to salute you or something." Vinnie smiled, but as he looked at the woman in the casket his smile faded. "Tell me something, Paul. Did you ever think of her when you were fighting? I was fighting a different kind of war in California, but thought about her every time I got mad enough to take off somebody's head. Instead of just letting my anger loose, I'd think of the old broad and I'd suck it up! Keeping my head under pressure was the most important thing I ever learned from her."

A tall thin blonde man with a bald spot on top of his head silently walked up to the casket just in time to hear Vinnie's words. "I also learned that lesson well," he casually remarked as he stared at Mrs. Chutney. "If I hadn't learned that lesson, I might have killed my old man. I could've been in prison now. She not only taught me how to suck it up, but how to let it go. That has helped me all my life."

"Whoa! You look like one of the Giovanni twins. Which one are you, Brian or Patrick?" Paul smiled as he recognized another high school buddy.

"I'm Brian. My brother was killed in a drive-by shooting while he was walking home not long after we graduated from high school. I still miss him everyday." He confessed. "All my old man could do at first was talk about what a loser Patrick was and how if we were in a gang we had to expect to be shot. Neither of us was ever in a gang. Mrs Chutney saw to that!"

He laughed a little bit. "But I came close to going after my old man when he wouldn't shut up about Patrick. I had to run out of the house. For some reason the first person I needed find was Mrs.Chutney. She inited me into her house and sat up with me all night She listened and quietly talked to me. She said people who lose loved ones, especially a child, always experience intense anger. She said my Pa's words were probably just that kind of anger coming out."

Brian continued. "She said it was common for people to blame something or someone when they lose a loved one and I was probably just handy. I calmed down and went home when the sun came up. I found my old man sitting in the living room sobbing, saying he was sorry and didn't mean what he'd said and he thought he's lost me too. It was very emotional, but we got to be a lot closer after that. Who would've thought that mean old broad was really such an angel?" He shook his head from side to side.

"What are you doing with yourself now? My Ma never mentioned you still living in Newark," Vinnie pointed out.

"I moved to New York City after college," Brian recalled. "I can still remember how much I hated math. Patrick and I were always kind of slow at math of any kind. We were afraid we'd never graduate because of it. Getting put into Mrs. Chutney's remedial math class was the best thing that ever happened to us. She convinced us we were math 'geniuses' and made us believe it."

He continued, "Once she found out we could speak Italian, Gaelic, and English, she said we should just think of mathematics as a language. She said it was just a short way of writing out very long ideas. It was always the same tense. There was no past or future tenses to remember, just the present. So Pat and I studied it like a language and I swear both of our grades shot right up to A's." Brian again shook his head from side to side.

"I have to admit, though, it took her a while to convince us we weren't just stupid trouble makers like a lot of teachers made us feel. But she sure didn't fool around with anyone slacking off! It was during that time she had me and Pat scared and mad at the same time until we thought she was a real b…" Brian quickly noticed the women nearby. "Uh, well, we thought she was such a witch, we plotted ways to get her!'

Brian laughed, "She was always way ahead of us, though. She is right up there along with my mother and my wife as a standard by which I judge all women. She was responsible for more than remediation. I earned my MBA in college and am now a stock broker on Wall Street."

He said bragging a bit, "I did that for my brother, my dad, my mom and for Mrs. Chutney. I don't know if she knew about it or not.

Paul looked Brian in the eye. "Oh, she knew about it, I'm sure. All the time I was fighting overseas she sent me cards and letters and little packages of things she thought I might need in the desert. She kept up with all her students I think."

"You're right!" Vinnie exclaimed. "Now I remember when I was faced with the hostile takeover for the company I'd built around my own inventions; she sent a funny card and wrote, "Hang in there, Boy." I don't know how she knew what I was going through at that time. It's still a mystery to me."

Vinnie's wife, Chloe, a tall, trim redhead with chocolate eyes, asked out of curiosity, "Why did you hate her? What makes all of you say she was so mean that you refer to her as 'old broad' and 'witch' and 'old lady'?"

All three of the men laughed out loud. It was Paul who finally answered her, "Mrs. Chutney taught remedial English, remedial Math, remedial Science, and was also apart-time coach in girls' gymnastics. She wasn't very big, but she was so strong, it was amazing. All the kids in her remedial classes, including us, were kind of the 'dregs' of the school. She got all the bullies and trouble makers in her classes."

He continued, "The first thing she did was make sure her students were listening during class. While she was teaching, she had a habit of walking up and down the aisles between the desks. Anyone who wasn't listening was pinched on the ear or smacked on the head or something. Sometimes she'd sneak up on someone sleeping in class and her voice would suddenly increase in volume right into the students ear. I'm telling you, her voice could get so loud you could hear her down the street!"

Vinnie also tried to describe Mrs. Chutney's unusual teaching methods, "This was a badass Newark High School and all the kids in her classes thought they were tough. However, it didn't take them long to learn who was the 'boss.' A lot of these kids were poor, with their parents out of work and to make matters worse they were being raised by single patents, too. These were usually the kids the teachers thought of as a 'waste of time.' They just wanted to get us through so we could go out in the world and take all the menial labor and service jobs around."

Vinnie continued, "After many years of being made to feel inferior to the rest of the world, I think all of us had 'bad attitudes' toward anybody in authority. Whenever we displayed a 'bad attitude' toward Mrs. Chutney, though, she really brought us down fast. The first time I remember her reacting to a bully was when big Boris Nochevsky stood up, grabbed her skinny little arm and brought back a big ham-like fist as if he were going to slug her."

"I can't swear to what she did," Vinnie exclaimed, "but it was lightning fast. The next thing we knew big Boris was flat on his back in the middle of the aisle. She put her foot hard against his neck and poked him with her wooden pointer in the stomach telling him, "If you ever again raise a hand to me, you'll wish you were dead. If you ever manage to hit me, you will be dead!" That was enough for me. Anytime she'd make me really angry by pushing me farther than I thought I could go, I learned to just suck it up and try harder."

Vinnie blew out a big sigh, "On the other hand, when we were good, she gave us all the praise and encouragement she could. Even big Boris brought his grades up in her classes."

Brian stood listening to his friends, trying to recall how he and his twin brother felt about Mrs. Chutney when they found themselves in her classes. "We'd heard lots of stories about her from other kids. We weren't sure all the stories were true. I mean, one of the first things we heard was that she once pulled some kid's arm completely off!"

Brian laughed, "But like you, we witnessed how she reacted to kids who tried to bully her. Patrick and I used to discuss ways we'd handle it if she ever hurt one or both of us. But one thing we both noticed was she never seemed to hold a grudge for the kids she had to 'straighten out' as she called it. Afterwards, she never made fun of them, but just went along as if nothing ever happened. She gave them the chance to behave and get back in her good graces."

He shook his head, "She forced us to listen and pay attention. When we got behind she would force us to stay after school for her tutoring. In fact she was late at school every night tutoring kids. She made you feel worthwhile. She was all business until we learned everything we needed to know."

"Whenever all of us passed a different exam for her, the next class would be a party! She'd smile and shout 'Woo-hoo!' as she passed out our test results. She'd tell us we were all wonderful and she wouldn't give us any homework that day. We got so we'd work hard just to have her pleased with us," Brian concluded.

Other people were coming up to the casket to pay their respects, so the five of them had to walk outside the funeral home.

"Are you guys going to the funeral tomorrow morning?"
Vinnie asked Paul and Brian. "I think I'll try to make it. Perhaps we can all go out to lunch afterwards and catch up?"

"That sounds like a great idea. Count me in." Brian agreed.

"Actually, I have to be there," Paul said quietly. "I've been asked to give the eulogy."

He noted their surprise, "I wasn't sure what I was going to say, but I got a lot of good ideas from the three of us remembering. And yes, I would be happy to meet you guys for lunch afterwards."

The following morning, Mrs Chutney looked peaceful lying in her casket at Sacred Heart Cathedral. She had taught high school for fifty years. It was a good thing her family chose to have her funeral in the largest Catholic church in Newark, New Jersey as the pews were filled. There wasn't even standing room because so many of her former students and colleagues came to say good bye.

Paul and his wife sat in front with Mrs. Chutney's family. When they introduced him as her 'former student,'Colonel Paul Rosini,' he walked up to the podium in his full-dress uniform and took a deep breath. He was saddened and angry that someone so important in his life was gone, but just as Mrs. Chutney had taught him, he sucked it up and let it go. He then felt quiet and calm.

It was as if Mrs. Chutney was there listening to him. Perfectly poised, he began,

"Mrs. Chutney was the toughest, meanest, scariest teacher I ever knew. She forced me to believe in myself. She forced me to be better than I thought I could be. She forced me to become my own hero. She wasn't just a teacher, she was an educator about life. I'll always love her for that."

At this, everyone in the church stood and applauded. All her students in attendance from the past knew exactly what he was talking about. It was a most fitting tribute to their beloved "old broad."

The Extra Child

I believe it sometimes does take a village to raise a child. It did for Kenny.

When I got pregnant with my first baby, my husband and I bought a small house in the Chicago suburbs. Shortly after I moved in, several women arrived with little girls and bakery goods to welcome me to the neighborhood. The women had different backgrounds, but they all shared one thing in common-desperation with a little neighbor boy named Kenny.

Kenny was the "Dennis the Menace" of the neighborhood. He was known to secretly ring people's doorbells constantly for days at a time. In the spring he pulled the flowers off people's tulips, hyacinths, and daffodils, so just the stems were left standing. He made crayon drawings on the sidewalks in front of several people's homes. He broke eggs in Mrs. Kowalski's mailbox, and he smeared thick mud across Mrs. Hernandez' bay window. He poured maple syrup all over Mrs. Warren's pristine prize-winning Angora cat, Precious. He also smeared cooking oil all over Mrs. Peterson's poor old German shepherd, Wolfie. He had caused a lot of aggravation for everyone at one time or another. I naturally asked if they had talked to his mother.

"Huh!" Mrs. Kowalski responded. She was an older woman with salt-'n'-pepper hair. She'd been an instructor for military pilots. She had put in her twenty years with the U.S. Air Force and was retired, but she still liked to fly her little Cessna. Her manner was what some called "down-to-earth."

"Mrs. Huntley is that skinny witch with the short dark hair and mean face. When she smiles, she always looks like she's being pinched. If you try to tell her about Kenny, she just slams the door in your face. She throws her kids out of that house first thing in the morning, rain or shine, and then she locks the doors so they can't get back in until she finishes her housework.

"Do you ever mention Kenny's behavior to his father?"

Mrs. Kowalski looked down and answered gruffly, "No, we don't."

Mrs. Warren, a mild young woman with long brown hair and Bambi eyes, tried to explain in her sweet way, "Kenny's a nuisance, but he's not really bad. He's never really broken anything. He's never actually hurt an animal or another child. I've even seen him hug smaller children who were crying. Once I saw him helping my own little girl get up after a fall. I went out and thanked him, telling him what a nice thing he did. He looked surprised, but he smiled. I don't remember him ever bothering Precious again after that."

Mrs. Warren raised purebred cats and Precious was a very expensive pussycat whose kittens were worth their weight in gold.

Mrs. Warren continued in a more somber tone, "I remember when the Huntley family first moved in, a few of us did tell Kenny's father on him. Each time someone did, Kenny didn't come out of his house for a week—and he was still bruised all over when he did. We never told on him again."

"My God! What kind of man is his father?"

Mrs. Kowalski replied, "Oh Mr. Huntley's friendly enough and you'll never see a bruise on his idiot-of-a-wife——just little Kenny. I don't know what goes on over there, but a little kid doesn't deserve that severe a punishment for pranks. We try to correct him ourselves in other ways—like I made him wash the crayon off my sidewalk with a special cleaner. Afterwards I said 'Good job' and gave him a homemade doughnut. I'd never tell on him."

Mrs. Peterson was the wife of a local Anglican minister. She was a perfectly groomed, very chic brunette with excellent diction. She worked for their church as a professional speaker and was good at fundraising. She visited the retired church members regularly and also checked on any sick members. She was known for her kindness, being well-educated, having perfect manners, and never gossiping—-with one exception:

I remember that appalling Mrs. Huntley once explained her 'problem' to me—and, mind you, she said this right in front of Kenny. She had wanted only two children, a boy and a girl. Her first was their son, Patrick. Her second was their daughter, Kimberly. However, Kimberly was bad-mannered enough to be born with a twin brother, who was apparently unexpected. Kenny was the 'extra child' she never wanted. Mrs. Huntley spoils and fawns all over Patrick and Kimberly, but she ignores Kenny. In fact, she hardly acknowledges the boy is hers."

Mrs. Peterson expressed her own conclusion about Mrs. Huntley in the vernacular, "She's a weirdo!"

Mrs. Hernandez' husband was a Mexican diplomat and she herself had been a primary school teacher until she started her own family. She was a pretty brunette with lively brown eyes. She loved children. She had four of her own with another one on the way She'd never once been overheard yelling at her kids. In fact, her children laughed all the time, just like she did.

"Once a week, when I know Kenny will be around, I hide by the side of the door when he rings the bell, I open the door quickly, hand him a bag of cookies, and then close the door again!" Mrs. Hernandez admitted. "It's a little game we play every Saturday morning. He's a smart little one, though, once when I opened the door, he immediately handed me an empty cookie bag!" She laughed, and then commented, "He actually left my spring flowers alone this year."

The Huntley's lived directly across the street from me. Next door to them lived a couple who would become my good friends, Anna and Gerhardt Braun. They had immigrated from Germany. Anna was a tall, athletic blonde woman who was a secretary for an import-export company. She had been an Olympic swimmer when she was young, so theirs was the only house in the subdivision with an Olympic sized swimming pool in the back yard. Anna was also the only woman in the neighborhood whom the infamous Kenny did not annoy with his tricks. I found why.

"Gerhardt and I have not been blessed with children yet, but we often play with the Huntley children next door. We've learned Patrick and Kimberly never get into trouble themselves, but they are 'tattletales.' They go crying to their mother every time Kenny looks at them the wrong way. Then he gets a beating, while they stand there looking smug."

"Kenny does things to annoy people. However, if you give him good attention, then he is your loyal friend forever. Compared to Kenny, the other two are like milk toast. Kenny is smarter, more spirited, and has twice as much personality as both of them put together. We adore him."

"Gerhardt and I also intervene when his father gets angry with him. His father goes too far with corporal punishment—especially to a six-year-old child. I remind him he could do permanent damage to the boy. Gerhardt tells him he must stop now or he'd better look out when that little boy is grown!"

One morning I was just getting ready to give my baby his breakfast when my doorbell rang. I opened the door but nobody was there. Then I remembered what the women had told me about Kenny, so I stepped outside to see if I could find him anywhere, I finally did. I spotted the pointed top of his snowsuit hood sticking out near the corner of my garage.

"Hi, you must be Kenny. Did you come over to introduce yourself?"

The pointed hood nodded yes.

"It's kind of cold outside today. Why don't you come inside and I'll make you some hot chocolate?"

A cute little blue-eyed boy with light brown hair, red cheeks and a big smile, minus two front teeth, walked away from the garage and entered my house.

I showed him to the kitchen and pointed to my baby in his carrier on the table. "This is my son, Bobby. Do you think you could feed him his cereal while I make our chocolate?"

"I don't know how." Kenny's face was frightened.

"In that case, I'd better show you what to do." I demonstrated how much cereal to put on the end of the baby spoon and how to carefully put it into the baby's mouth, gently scooping up what fell out.

"He's just a little baby. He doesn't yet know how to move his tongue so the food goes in, not out, getting all over him—see."

We both laughed when little Bobby pushed most of his cereal out of his mouth with his tongue while trying to eat it. I allowed Kenny to show me if he thought he could do it. He was very patient and fed the baby exactly as I'd shown him.

"Wow! I think you did it better than I did my first time. You'll make an excellent daddy someday."

Kenny's face looked very pleased when I complimented him.

I gave the boy his hot chocolate in a grown-up mug like mine and made myself some tea. I also put toast with strawberry jam on the table. We had a nice chat while I gave Bobby his bottle, then I changed him and put him down for his nap.

"Can I feed Bobby his cereal again?"

"Sure—while I make you hot chocolate."

"OK! I'll see you tomorrow." Kenny waved goodbye.

That's how our unique friendship began. It lasted another five years until I moved away. I enjoyed Kenny's company immensely. We talked about all sorts of things. I learned a lot about a child's point of view from him. I like to think our friendship was good for Kenny, too. After that morning, I never had another complaint about him from the neighbors.

Anna and Gerhardt were still friends with the Huntley family after I moved away, so Anna gave me updates from time to time. Mr. and Mrs. Huntley were having trouble in their marriage. All three of the children grew to be taller than their parents, so it was fortunate Mr. Huntley took Gerhardt's advice and stopped beating Kenny. He told Gerhardt in confidence he also stopped because his wife stopped speaking to him. Consequently, he no longer had to listen to her badgering him to punish the boy as soon as he'd get home form work. Mr. Huntley said he quit hitting Kenny altogether because he felt guilty. He figured out he was actually angry with his wife, not his son. He began to pay more attention to Kenny because he noticed his wife never did.

Mr. Huntley and Kenny became closer as father and son. When the Huntley's finally separated, Patrick and Kimberly begged to live with their mother. Kenny chose to live with his father. Huntley had paid attention to Kenny—and learned Anna was right. The boy was absolutely devoted to him. Unlike his siblings, it was Kenny, the 'extra chid' who graduated with honors from high school and went to college on a scholarship.

When Kenny grew up, he took a job which moved him to California. I never heard of him after that, but I sometimes think back to when he was a little boy. I remember how much of his mischief the neighbors put up with before they'd ever tell his parents. Most of them tried to pay as much attention to him as they could in friendly little ways. A few of us became trusted adults to Kenny.

A little kindness is a small investment that can often result in big dividends. Kenny is proof of that.

Yvonne C. Hebert, MA, worked for thirty years as a psychotherapist with individuals and families in California. Her career has included positions as a social worker with Michigan Children's Services and as a Rehabilitation Counselor in S. California. She completed training in Spiritual Direction at Mt. St. Mary's College in Los Angeles. She has been active in several L.A. parishes as a Eucharistic Minister, Group Leader, and Counselor. She is a Dominican Associate with the Grand Rapids, MI., Dominicans. She studied creative writing at UCLA.

Forgiveness and Trust

Recently at a speaking engagement, a member of the audience told me of going to a lecture on forgiveness where the psychologist lecturer said that when a person truly forgives, they also trust again. I would disagree with this statement.

Make no mistake about this fact. Trust is not a component of forgiveness. Let's discuss who is responsible for each activity. The injured party is responsible for forgiving which is an internal emotional and mental adjustment to a situation over which they have no control. The offending party is responsible for the behavior which created the situation. If their behavior does not change, it would be foolhardy for the injured party to trust them again. If their behavior does change, it will take time for this to be apparent to other people, including the forgiving party.

Forgiveness changes the forgiver. It gives them an internal peace, strengthens their character, and gives them a deeper understanding of human beings around them. It does not change their vulnerability to someone insulting them a second time.

To forgive another person does not mean that one must trust that person again. It does not mean that you condone their behavior and it does not mean that you agree with them. The only way to change an offender's behavior is to directly confront the offender and make them aware of the results of their behavior and how offensive it was to the other party. Then, perhaps, the offender may wish to alter their behavior, but there is no guarantee that they will make changes.

Behavior is addictive, its comfortable, it's the way we're used to being and amending our behavior takes determination, courage, and motivation. Depending on their relationship, they may wish to continue interacting with each other. For trust to develop the offender will need to show behavioral adjustments over time.

Forgiveness is for the offended person. It breaks the negative tie between the two people which have been put in place by the offensive behavior. This damaging connection continues due to the energy the offended party gives to it. When the offended party stops the flow of energy to their thoughts about the situation, stops wishing for more respectful behavior from the other person and stops wanting an apology, the energy chain between the two people is broken and forgiveness happens.

Forgiveness means that you are allowing the other person to be who they are and you are not going to attempt to control them, or to demand apologies, or judge them. You are going to release them to be responsible for their own behavior and attitudes, and you are going to do what you need to do to live peacefully and productively on the same planet where they live.

Trusting another person means to place your safety in their care. It means to believe that they will not willfully hurt you or prevent you from getting your personal needs satisfied. It means that you believe they will be responsible in their interactions with you and live up to the boundaries that the culture has accepted as normal.

These boundaries may be as neutral as the drivers of vehicles respecting the laws of the road that keep their respective cars and occupants safe as they travel. It may be as intimate as spouses maintaining the confidences their partner has shared with them, either verbally or physically.

It may be as dispassionate as people in a public place assuming the people around them will proceed with their business in an impartial, non-violent manner. It may be as cautious as two individuals meeting, hoping to begin a friendship, assuming the other person will be respectful of their needs and person.

The person who offends another does not change because they have been forgiven. They remain responsible for their behavior, which is a pattern of their life. They are unlikely to modify their behavior because someone has forgiven them for something they may not even know they've done.

The offended person is then able to release the offender to their responsibility for the insult. This has nothing to do with trust. Trust is not a component of forgiveness. Forgiveness does not imply that you trust the other person, that you agree with their position, that you condone their position, or that your relationship will continue. It does mean that you have broken the emotional chains that bind your mind to rehearsing the event and feeling the pain of the event repeatedly throughout your life.

An excerpt from "RETHINKING FORGIVENESS: MENTAL TACTICS TO AVOID RESENTMENT" by Yvonne C. Hebert, Published in 2013

THE POTTY BOX STANDOFF

Pandora was a neat, clean cat, fastidious about grooming her long orange fur. She was not given to eating a bite more than she needed. Her discipline amazed me since I often ate for the sheer pleasure of eating. On this particular morning, we had eaten breakfast about the same time and while I washed dishes and cleaned up the kitchen, she retired to a window sill to groom herself for the day.

When the kitchen was in order, I went into the bathroom to prepare for my day. Pandora followed me to the doorway, sat down regally, and watched me, her gold eyes observant and serious. As I unfastened my jeans, she walked casually into the room and, still watching me, stood on the tiny pink flowered rug in front of the wash basin. When I started to sit down, she turned her back to me, reached out a long arm and started dragging the rug toward herself.

I watched with disbelief as she pulled the mat into a pile. My disbelief turned to horror as she wiggled her little behind into the mounded folds of carpet. I knew beyond a shadow of a doubt that she was going to use the heaped up rug for a litter box.

"No," I shouted, leaping to my feet. Holding my clothes with one hand, I grabbed her around the abdomen, lifted her up against myself, and made a dash for her potty box which I had placed in a corner of my much larger bedroom.

I set her down on her litter, but she was having none of it. She made an unbelievable twist of her body, her little feet scattering bits of clay across the floor, flipped herself around and raced back down the hall toward the bathroom.

I couldn't believe my eyes but I knew she was going back to use the carpet. I chased after her down the hall and reached the bathroom just as she was again wiggling her bottom into the comfortable folds she had arranged.

"No," I said sternly, reaching for her. "You know better than this! What's the matter with you?"

I grabbed her up again, gave her a little shake and raced down the hall to her potty box. By this time, I could feel the energy that was pulsing between us. Her muscles were tensing with energy and she was feeling much heavier than she had just a moment before.

As I lowered her down to her litter, her muscles seemed to explode in my hands. Her back feet caught the rim of the potty box and she gave it a mighty kick. It skittered several inches across the floor as she burst out of my hands. I watched her galloping back down the hall to the bathroom and felt totally astonished.

My mind raced through the implications of what was happening and I came to an instant conclusion.

"I'm smarter than any cat," I told myself. "She is going to use this litter box and not that rug."

I reached down, grabbed the potty box and chased her down the hall with it, arriving just as she was, again, making her bottom secure in the rumpled folds of pink flowers.

Letting go of my clothes, I grabbed her up with one hand while I slid the potty box under her with the other. It wobbled precariously but I dropped her onto it anyway.

She did her business quickly, and with the box tipping under her weight she quite efficiently covered the spot, sniffed it once and stepped out onto the crumpled rug. Walking with great dignity to the bathroom door, her tail straight up behind her, the tip flipping slightly, she glanced up at me briefly before disappearing into the hallway.

Her look was not mean or challenging. It was not gloating or happy. It was just a look, but I got the message.

"You're really slow, Lady, but you did manage to get there."

I pulled my jeans up from around my ankles and considered the situation. She wanted her potty box in the bathroom where people did their business. She wasn't wrong in what she wanted.

I knew that it would be less trouble to find a way to keep her litter box in the crowded bathroom than to put it back in the bedroom. This wasn't a fight I wanted to have again.

Her box stayed where it was, and from then on, when anyone was using the apartment conveniences, she often joined that person for some mutual relief.

On occasion after that, I wondered how many times, and in how many ways, she had tried to let me know that she wanted the location of her bathroom moved. If nothing else, this confrontation had proven to me that she had the capacity for deep feelings about her life and what she liked and didn't like.

I promised myself that I would try to be more observant of her efforts to communicate with me in the future. It just might forestall another battle such as that which we had just been through! I really hated losing a mental battle to a cat!

Many years in the future, Pandora and I would butt heads about potty issues again, but for the time being peace reigned.

An excerpted from "Pandora" By Yvonne C. Hebert To be published in 2018

Della Helton shared the following: "I was sure excited when Randy Johnston invited me to attend the Write to Publish group she belonged to. I like to write, but had only written for our herb group, or the Michigan Herb Association Journal.

Randy and the others inspired me, that perhaps someday I could really publish a book. One day Randy brought this into the Write to Publish meeting. It was so exiting to read this man's story."

'An extraordinary story is proving you are never too old to learn new things. A ninety-eight year old man, Jim Henry, in Connecticut has come out with his first book. He was illiterate until the age of ninety-six. He decided to learn to read and write so he could tell his stories as Sea Captain for almost fifty years. For most of Jim's life he couldn't even spell his own name. Now he is signing his own books!'

"There is still hope for me," Della said. "I am only going to be seventy-eight years old this year.

Blueberry Picking

    I was excited as I climbed into my old Ford Bronco. I was going to spend the weekend with Aunt Marge at her place on the Muskegon River. We were going to be visiting relatives, blueberry picking and cooking for the entire weekend.

    Aunt Marge made the best fried chicken and biscuits, and her pies were so yummy! This weekend she was going to help me to learn the secrets of her great cooking. I loved visiting with her, as she was raised by the same Grandma I was. She is twenty years older than I am, and so much fun to be with and so very wise.

    When I got to Auntie's house she had everything ready to go, and we were going in her new, fancy Oldsmobile car. First we would do our visiting, then tomorrow we will be blueberry picking and cooking the rest of the weekend.

    Everything went fine, we had such a grand time visiting relatives but it caused us to get a late start going home. Aunt Marge said we'll take the back way through the woods, as it was faster. We were almost back to her house when Aunt Marge said she might wet her pants and was going to have to stop and go behind the car. Now I was not really comfortable with this idea, it was getting dark out, and *gosh* anything could be out in these woods!

    I couldn't talk her out of it. She stopped, put the car in park and jumped out. Frantically I looked around and saw headlights in the distance. *Oh no*, I must let Aunt Marge know! So, I thought I would roll down the window and holler. But which button was it?

Well, the first one put my seat back and the next one locked the doors. By this time Auntie is banging on the rear door to let her in, but I couldn't seem to find the right button. Now poor Aunt Marge is hiding behind the car to stay out of the approaching headlights. *Oh my gosh*, my seat is going up and down, forward and backward, for a minute it reminded me of a carnival ride!

Finally, I hit the right button and Aunt Marge got in. The car had passed us by and kept on going, thank God. Aunt Marge was hopping mad, "Della, how could you do such a silly thing?"

I tried to explain my old Ford Bronco didn't have all those silly buttons. I was scared so I was hitting them all. Well, Auntie didn't speak the rest of the way home. I thought, this fun weekend just ended. No blueberry picking tomorrow and no cooking fried chicken. And no pies!

We pulled into the drive and Aunt Marge told me to get my PJ's on and it was time to go to bed. We would not be playing cards. Well, at least I knew I was invited to stay another night.

In the morning I awoke to the smell of fried chicken and biscuits. And there stood Aunt Marge, smiling, with our buckets in hand ready to go berry picking. All is forgiven.

Peggy Hoard, has written poetry and stories beginning in high school and news articles for years. She has poems published in Eber & Wein books: *In My Lifetime* and *Best Poets of 2015*. She currently has two books published through Create Space: *Christmas Skits for Churches,* which contains complete Christmas skits and prop directions for six to eight years, and *Questions,* a true story relating the events after she received a telephone informing that her son had been shot. She tells how she had to find a way to forgive the deceased ones involved and continue to live.

At funerals she writes a personal poem about the deceased one's life, reads it at the funeral and presents it to the survivors.

She was raised in Marion, Michigan and graduated from Marion High School. In 2002, after retirement, she and her husband purchased the land and homestead where she was raised. Her mother still resided in the home and they were able to have her with them for fifteen years, until her death.

Peggy enjoys writing and participating in writing groups." It is gratifying to watch writers grow in their skill and some, become published. Writing is a true journey, and a journey to enjoy."

The Case

Jenny was excited to try her first case as defense attorney. Bill, the former Defense Attorney had died of a heart attack just a month prior. Since she had been working closely with him on this case, well, the job instantly fell to her.

Thirty-two years old, single, a figure to die for, long blonde hair, and sky blue eyes drew many interesting looks. She owned her own three bedroom ranch house and a candy apple red Ford Mustang. Oh yeah, she definitely looked and felt on top of the world.

Jared was such a nice young man. He graduated from Harvard with a degree in accounting/finances. Tall, dark and handsome described him quite well. His short cropped raven hair and green eyes captivated Jenny's attention at first glance.

His mom and dad both held executive jobs. Money didn't seem to be a problem as they had fully paid for Jared's five years of college and were paying his hefty attorney fees. They both believed their son was completely innocent.

Jenny parked at the court house and sat in silence. Mary had accused Jared of kidnaping, torture and rape, but Jenny couldn't believe he was guilty. He was so polite in manner and speech, soft in tone, and quick to hold the chair for her. No, she was right. Jared was innocent and she was going to prove it.

It made her sick how many young girls accused boys of raping them, when in fact they were willing and able. When they became pregnant or caught-it suddenly became rape.

Mary didn't seem trustworthy anyway. She was always whining in a high pitch voice and cried whenever you looked at her. She was a senior in high school, unpopular, but a very good student. Her family was very poor and on welfare. She probably had sex with some high schooler she had a crush on and then blamed Jared, hoping to weasel money from his parents.

The trial lasted four long, stressful days. On day one Jenny drilled Mary with every personal question she could think of. Had she dated, did she have a boyfriend, hadn't she flirted with Jared, and on and on. She badgered her, accused her, degraded and shamed her. Numerous times the trial was recessed to allow Mary to compose herself.

Day three she looked exhausted. Her eyes were red and puffy. Her voice had become weak and more squeaky. Jenny knew she Mary was close to breaking down and was sure she would confess that the sex with Jared was consensual.

Jared was always composed and when Mary would state that he had raped and tortured her, he would lower his head and slowly shake it side to side. The prosecuting attorney drilled him over and over, yet he always gave the same answers; Mary had pursued him, she had requested to have sex, she was mad when he wouldn't buy her the things she wanted.

He stayed calm and looked hurt that she would accuse him of such brutality.

With the trial over the decision was now in the jury's hands. Jared left he courtroom with his parents. They were smiling, laughing and his dad was patting him on the back while his mother locked her arm in his.

Mary left alone, in fact, Jenny realized she had never seen her parents, friends or other family in the court room. Her shoulders were drooped, head lowered as she daubed her eyes. Jenny couldn't feel sympathy for her. She knew she was lying. Little poor girl trying to dig a way out of poverty so she goes after the rich boy.

Three days later they were called to the courthouse, as the jury had reached a verdict. Jared looked impeccable in his dark blue suit, mauve shirt and stripped tie. Mary was dressed in a well worn summer dress, and once again alone. Jared stood as the verdict was read. Innocent echoed in
the room. His parents whooped for joy as Jared hugged Jenny. His parents thanked her profusely.

Mary wiped tears from her face as she slowly walked out of court. She looked so devastated, but she still couldn't feel sympathy for the liar.

Two days later Jenny was informed that Mary had jumped off the Kingston Bridge, forty feet into the swift river. She was dead.

"Well," Jenny thought, "I guess she just couldn't live with the lies."

Three weeks later as Jenny exited her car at home, a cloth soaked with chloroform was placed over her mouth and nose. When she awoke she found her hands were tied overhead by a rope suspended from a rusty water pipe, tape over her mouth and totally naked. She screamed, but only muffled noise escaped.

The door creaked open and Jared walked in. Jenny's eyes grew large in disbelief.

Jared smiled brightly: "Ah, my beautiful attorney. Welcome to my parlor. Let the fun begin!"

Does She Know I Care?

She softly closed her eyes, lowered her head and slowly swayed it side to side. Change was hard, especially change into the unknown.

My heart tightened with guilt and understanding. To her I was placing her somewhere she didn't want to be.

In the past three months she had been taken to the hospital due to bad falls resulting in injuries. Twice she had been taken directly from the hospital to a rehab facility. Now with her insurance coverage at an end, a decision had to be made. I couldn't consider a nursing home, as her mind was so sharp, it was just her mobility that was causing the trouble.

She desperately wanted to come home. Home? Yes, the home she and her husband had built, raised their three children in, the farm they had maintained for over sixty years. The same place my husband and I purchased fifteen years ago. She had come with the package as she was still living there. For the next fifteen years we were able to have her with us.

Now everything had changed. Her last fall removed the skin off the top of her right arm from the wrist almost to the elbow, several lacerations on the hand, skin off the elbow to the bone and a bad contusion to the right side of her face. She was required to be where there was twenty-four-hour care.

The words "I told you so" echoed in my ears. Twice before the doctors had told me NOT to bring her home. It was no longer safe for her to be left alone, and impossible for my husband and me to be home all the time. Twice I didn't listen. I was sure we could manage.

However, my husband was recovering from a three-way-bypass and restricted to lifting no more than five pounds. It was extremely hard on him not to be able to help her when she needed assistance.

Twice more she fell and was injured. Now the doctors insisted that she be placed in either an assisted living or nursing home.

I had stopped at the assisted living home prior to picking her up from the nursing home. I brought her own pillow, sheets, bed spread and clothes. I was hopeful that when she saw her own things that she would feel more at home.

Wheeling her inside I watched her carefully. She was afraid, unsure. Change was so difficult for her. She watched as I put her clothes in the dresser and closet. I felt her watching my every move. My heart tightened. My mind screamed, *It's not my choice Mom. I don't want you here. The doctors have insisted that I'm harming you if I bring you home again!*

"Look Mom, a sunroom right by your bed. There's a skylight letting in the sun and all kinds of flowers and plants, recliners and even an electric fireplace!"

No response, she still held her head down. *Dear God*, I silently prayed, *help me to be strong. Help her to accept.*

"Do you want to go into the living room and meet the other ladies and find out who your two roommates are?"

She shook her head no and continued to look down. My eyes filled with tears and my heart tightened into a painful ball. The guilt I felt is hard to describe. I too felt helpless and hopeless. I turned away to dry my tears.

After several minutes, "I guess I might as well go out there. I have to meet them sooner or later."

A little flicker of hope entered my heart.

"Oh Mom, there are ladies you know there. Your neighbor for years, Barb, is here."

No response, her head was still down, hands folded in her lap. My mind screamed, *It's not what I want Mom, I want you home!*

Would she ever understand how much I loved her and that she was here because I cared?

A Twinkle in His Eye

Chatters of delight could be heard all along Main Street in Cottersville. The time was almost nine am, when Mr. Emerson would unlock the doors to his department store. A line of children kept warm by stomping their feet in a line that wound around the block one and a half times.

Mrs. Darwood, manager of the Timberland Orphanage, ten miles out of town, had been standing in line since seven forty-five that morning. With her were eight of her orphan girls from five to thirteen years old. They shivered in the cold, partly in eager anticipation to see Santa for the first time and tell him their Christmas wish. Every year in July, the Timberland orphans exchanged places with Hillside orphans from Millersburg because the Board of Directors believed exchanging the girls' residence would give them a better chance for adoption.

Mrs. Darwood wasn't thrilled to fix breakfast at five-thirty, nor stand in the cold for two hours, but one look at the girls' faces made her grumpiness melt away.

Thirteen-year-old Patty scraped frost off the Emerson store window with the cuff of her worn and faded coat. Suddenly, she let out a high shriek and exclaimed, "Mr. and Mrs. Santa Claus just came in!"

Five-year-old Becky and Jackie discovered they were too short to see through the window, and begged for details.

"Well," said Patty, "Mr. Claus is dressed in red velvet, trimmed in white fur. His hair is white; he has a long, thick white beard, and he wears gold wire-rimmed glasses. He's sitting in a huge black chair right now. Oh, and he has shiny black boots - so shiny you can almost see yourself in them."

"Tell us more, Patty," begged Becky.

"Mrs. Claus has a container of candy canes and a plate of cookies. Her red velvet dress is trimmed with white fur that looks so soft you could bury your face in it. Oh my, her hair is white as snow. She's swept it up in a thick bun. She has a beautiful round face with blushing cheeks and the most beautiful smile I've ever seen, and she wears the same gold wire rimmed glasses as Mr. Clause."

Jackie pulled on Patty's sleeve. "More, Patty, tell me more!"

"Well, let me see. Mr. Emerson is behind the counter getting the cash register ready. Mrs. Emerson is in the back, rearranging toys on long wooden shelves."

Village children edged closer to see through the window. Mrs. Darwood was quick to intervene. "Now, now, children, let's not cut in line. Please wait your turn. The store will open in a couple more minutes."

The orphans breathed a sigh of relief as the village children moved back, because their time was limited; they had to return to the orphanage soon and do chores. They could also sense looks of disgust on the faces of mothers who pointedly examined their faded and patched coats and boots. The girls were happy with what they did have, though; Mrs. Darwood had knitted each of them new mittens, hats, and scarves, clothing that looked much warmer than the store-bought garments other children were wearing. They didn't allow the narrow-minded women to dampen their spirits.

Suddenly Barbara grabbed Sally's shoulders. "Look," she said, "Mr. Emerson's coming from behind the counter and getting his key out!"

You could feel the excitement in the air. It seemed like everyone was talking at once. For a moment, there was silence; the key was inserted, turned, and then the door opened. Orphans rushed to form a line in front of Santa. Laughter and chatter filled the room. Heat from the huge pot-bellied stove felt so good on their cold skin. And when they smelled the cookies Mrs. Claus had prepared for them, their stomachs tightened.

"Good morning, young girls and boys," said Mrs. Claus. "Merry Christmas! I made these cookies fresh last night. Chocolate chip with extra chips and walnuts. Please take a candy cane and cookie before you leave."

Patty gently pushed Becky and Jackie to the front. Becky approached Santa first. He slowly lifted her onto his lap. His eyes twinkled and his smile was so welcoming.

"Well, my precious child, what would you like Santa to bring you for Christmas?"

Becky looked into his eyes and motioned for him to come closer. Then she whispered in his ear. In turn he whispered back. She laughed with joy as he gently lifted her down from his lap and stood her on the floor.

Jackie was next. She followed Becky's example, filling the air with laughter as delightful as a delicate wind chime singing in the wind.

Six-year-old Sally was next, followed by Annie, seven; then Debby, eight; Mary, ten; Barbara, eleven; and Patty, thirteen, completing the group. They fell in love with Mr. and Mrs. Claus, especially Mrs. Claus, who fit the model the girls had dreamed of when yearning for their own mothers.

Mr. and Mrs. Claus spent extra time with the orphan girls. You could tell the orphans held a particularly special place in their hearts, and in the Emerson's as well, perhaps because both couples were childless.

Mr. and Mrs. Emerson laughed along with the milling people, invited them to browse and discover all the merchandise.

For the past five years, John and Martha Littlefield had been employed to play Mr. and Mrs. Claus. The Emersons were pleased with them; they arrived early and willingly stayed late; they dressed beautifully, and had just the right personalities for their roles. Mr. Emerson-knew other companies had tried to bribe them away, so he paid them well to remain exclusively at his store. What's more, they remained faithful.

    Mr. Emerson loved this time of year, when everyone was in a festive mood and sales were high. He remained behind the counter watching the parade of children arrive. Mrs. Claus greeted every child with a kind smile and a tender voice that sounded much the way an Angel might sound. After each child finished telling Santa what they wanted, Mrs. Claus gave him or her the warmest hug she could, along with a candy cane and a homemade cookie. If children shoved or tried to cut in front of someone, she quickly let them know that Santa would put them on the naughty list and the behavior stopped immediately.

    Mr. Emerson watched Santa. He was so patient and gentle with the children. His continual Ho, Ho, Ho's filled the air with excitement. He never rushed a child, nor complained if they looked too old or heavy for his lap. Yes, Mr. Emerson was well pleased to employ this couple as Mr. and Mrs. Claus. He was even more satisfied when parents purchased their child's gifts from his store. Business was great; he credited the Clauses for the majority of his success. He would often tell his wife, "If only more people were like them, the world would be a far, far better place."

    It was March of the following year when the State Police knocked on the Littlefield's door. Mrs. Littlefield broke into tears when they handcuffed Mr. Littlefield, again when they took him away, and again at six o'clock the next morning when the news reported how he was charged with multiple counts of child molestation.

    Months later the full story was revealed; for several years, after each Christmas, Mr. Littlefield would take the orphan girls, one by one, to his house for dinner. Then, when taking them back to the orphanage, would stop and molest them. It had been happening with different girls for over five years.

At the trial each girl told how they loved Mrs. Littlefield, aka Mrs. Claus, and how she cooked them a wonderful meal, then gave them a handmade quilt and other gifts. Mr. Littlefield, aka Mr. Claus, threatened them not to tell Mrs. "Claus" Littlefield because her heart would break, and cause her to die of a heart attack. The orphans kept silent to avoid hurting her. With the older girls, he simply threatened to harm the younger ones if they told. Out of fear and shame, they too kept silent.

However, things changed when young Patty became pregnant. Mrs. Darwood knew she hadn't been anywhere near a boy, and through questioning Patty in tender tones and assuring words, she learned about Mr. Littlefield. One by one, the other girls came forward and told what he had done to them. Mrs. Darwood called the State Police.

The State Police came right away and talked with the girls. They also contacted other orphans who had resided at Mrs. Darwood's during the past five years to determine if Mr. Littlefield had molested them and to obtain their testimonies. Indeed, Mr. Littlefield had preyed upon the majority of these girls. He thought he would not be discovered since every year the girls were traded with the other orphanages.

The rest is history. The dear, sweet, kind and loving Mr. Claus was actually a pervert who preyed upon vulnerable little girls who were deprived of their parents.

Mr. Emerson discontinued hiring a new Mr. and Mrs. Claus at his store. In fact, he felt so responsible for the tragedies that one year later, he hung himself in the store basement.

Mrs. "Claus" Littlefield moved away right after the trial. Her heart was broken. She truly had no idea what had been taking place. The court granted her custody of seven orphan girls, including Barbara, Mary, Sally, Annie, Debby, Jackie and Becky, and she moved to another-state where the little family could make a fresh start.

Mr. "Claus" Littlefield was stabbed to death in the prison yard two years later, falling prey to inmates with little tolerance for those who abuse or molest children.

Mrs. Emerson adopted Patty, and while they raised her baby daughter, Hope, Patty's business skills helped the amazed woman with her retail business. Alone, they were vulnerable. Together, they were a huge success.

The Honor of Veterans

When I see our red, white and blue flag waving with glory,
  My eyes fill with tears for both the told and untold stories.
For thousands who have suffered & died for our freedom,
  For our Veterans alive today whom we think of so seldom.
For parents who send their child off to boot camp with pride,
  Waving rapidly while wiping tears they're trying to hide.
How great the sacrifice the entire family & friends make.
  All in the name of our country & for our freedom's sake.
When we pass service personnel do we look the other way?
  Are we uncomfortable or uneasy not knowing what to say?
Try to visualize your son or daughter you are passing by,
  Take notice, be bold, approach them, no longer be shy.
Instead, look them straight in the eye & sincerely smile,
  Stop what you're doing & take time to chat for a while.
Say, "I will pray for you & your safety each & every day."
  Make him or her a little prouder to serve in the great USA.
On Memorial Day, shouldn't we always make the time,
  To participate in honoring our fallen comrades, so fine?
To stand at attention when our faithful Veterans march by?
  Salute the flag & bow our heads when they fire to the sky?
When the wreath is presented in memory of those lost at sea.

And others at the chosen grave-by getting down on a knee,
If the Veterans in the parade are into their retirement age,
　Shouldn't we ask where the younger Veteran's are today?
And wonder if their commitment to Memorial Day is lost?
　Don't they remember their military years and the cost?
Or is it our lack of appreciation for them they can see?
　Inhibiting them from being recognized as they should be?
Oh, it is such a small sacrifice for you to make a vow to do,
　And it wouldn't take a lot of time or energy from you.
Stop, hold out your hand to service personal you may greet.
　Thank them for serving and you hope you'll again meet.
Go to your area's Memorial Day Parade each year.
　Let the Veterans see your honor, support & emotional tear.
When raising your children & grandchildren with care,
　Teaching them to be kind to others & how to share,
To grow & learn from defeat & loss right from the start,
　To love & believe in the Lord Jesus with all of their heart,
Please, educate them on the importance of Memorial Day,
　To be thankful for the Veterans in an honoring way,
Forgetting not the sacrifices each one of them have made,
　The unconditional prices they, for us, have dearly paid.
If their vital importance isn't passed on by you & me,
　They will become a mere ledger instead of a living legacy.
So when you see a Veteran, or service personal, please say,
　"Thank you for fighting for our freedom and the USA."

G. James Link

I began my journey as a writer at age eleven when selected to be my patrol's scribe in Boy Scout Troop 164, sponsored by Lincoln Elementary School PTA. Throughout elementary school, junior high and high school—I didn't realize it at the time—but I had the good fortune to have English teachers who enjoyed making their students write. While stationed aboard aircraft carriers during my U.S. Navy enlistment, I often shared impressions of my visits to foreign ports of call around the Mediterranean Sea and North Atlantic Ocean, with friends and family. My dad commented that after reading several of my letters I should become a writer. Four years later I enrolled in Jackson Community College where I thrived academically studying under great teachers, eventually earning an Associate of Science degree. Before transferring to a four-year institution, I took a one-year sabbatical spending the summer bicycling from south-central lower Michigan to the Pacific northwest coast at Seattle, Washington.

I returned to study at Central Michigan University for three years while working summers in Boy Scout and Youth Conservation Corps camps in Michigan, Wisconsin and Utah, setting a course that would eventually lead me to live and work in Alaska for twenty-three years. Employment with the Bureau of Land Management and Alaska Department of Fish & Game enabled me to return to academia at the University of Alaska—Anchorage, to pursue secondary education teaching credentials and prepare for teaching architecture, building construction, computer assisted drafting, geology, and other high school science courses.

Over the many semesters writing for college class assignments and for my own classroom students, has helped develop and refine my thinking and writing abilities. Since the late 1990's, I've had articles published in the Michigan Industrial Technology Education Society Journal, interviews with prominent and up-and-coming banjo players in Banjo Newsletter, and inspirational accounts in church newsletters. Currently I'm working on finishing a book chronicling my summer bicycle journey and envisioning other titles I'd like to write. Remember—we *ALL* have a story, and nobody will read YOUR story if YOU don't write it!

My 58-Hour Total Solar Eclipse Journey of 2017

2017 Total Solar Eclipse

The beams of the headlights disappeared as I turned off the ignition switch. Opening the driver's side door I was engulfed by an ambient air temperature above 80 degrees F combined with humidity well above percent. The change was stifling after the eleven-hour trip inside an air-conditioned vehicle.

Black night sky revealed pin points of light originating as distant stars while cicada's whirred overhead in the Chinese elm tree, interrupting the stillness. Their high-pitched, continuous buzzing reminded me of dozens of chain saws working in the distance. It was a welcome sound after the 600 miles of Interstate highways my friend Dean and I had just traveled from Lansing, Michigan, to rural Murphysboro, Illinois. As we made the right turn from Illinois 127 onto a narrow black top road, I looked for numbers on a mailbox corresponding to those on an e-mail I received the day before. And there they were. Turning right on the long gravel driveway, I glanced at the dashboard digital clock. The time was just about midnight Central Standard Time. Continuing past the old farmhouse, a detached garage, and four parked vehicles, I stopped behind an orange Kubota tractor equipped for mowing grass.

All was quiet as the owners and their other guests slept. I removed my tent, sleeping pad, and essential gear from the rear of the low-slung Volkswagon Passat wagon. Using Dean's small flashlight, I found a fairly flat spot to pitch my two-person no-see-um netting tent.

I hurriedly unzipped the door and rolled out my pad inside, hoping to prevent any blood-sucking insects from making a meal of me once I had settled in for the night. Soon I had brushed my teeth and was ready for sleep. I returned to the tent and tried to make a swift entrance, first turning out the light to discourage the attraction of any flying insects while the open was door, and quickly zipped it closed behind me.

Laying out a clean sheet on top of the pad, I was more than ready to lie down, pulling another sheet over me. Dean was sleeping in his vehicle on a seat that reclined to nearly horizontal. We would be fortunate if the temperature dropped into the 70's before morning.

Waking as dawn began to break, illuminating the eastern horizon with subtle shades of yellows and gray-blue, I noticed the sound of cicadas had diminished overnight. The leaves on the trees barely moved in the stillness. My digital thermometer registered 79 degrees F briefly before its climb back up into the 80s. Rolling over, I drifted back to sleep.

An hour passed and a slight breeze coaxed me from the ripstop nylon shelter to begin this remarkable day. The owners had just left home for their day jobs at the local university, leaving Mary's parents to baby-sit their two young boys. Dean and I had to locate the nearest Volkswagon dealership and inquire about a repair to his vehicle, so were able to get an early start after meeting Mary's parents and getting the lowdown on the total solar eclipse viewing at the farm later that morning. The nearest dealership was in another town to the east about a half hour drive. After the mechanic's evaluation, we were directed to leave Dean's car and take a "loaner" until the defective part could be ordered and the repair completed the following morning. Unpacking our gear from his car and re-packing in the smaller loaner went quickly.

Once on the road again, we drove through Carbondale to find "total eclipse mania" alive, well, and in full capitalistic mode. It was about 10:00 am and folks were sitting on blankets on the grass along the sidewalks waiting to view the much-heralded August 21st, 2017 solar eclipse. Other folks were sitting on lawn chairs in city parks with tripods, cameras, telescopes and binoculars. Vendors were hawking T-shirts, mugs, eclipse glasses, hats, drinks and food. Vehicle parking spaces for all the hundreds of out-of-towners were advertised for $20.00!

The university stadium was set up to view the eclipse on its electronic scoreboard, charging admission for bleacher seating; many folks had filed in to take advantage of this electronic rendition of one of Creation's most spectacular astronomical events. The message on at least two church announcement signs we drove past, read, "God made the Sun and the Moon!" giving God the Creator the glory for His exquisitely planned and operating universe.

By the time we returned to the farm it was about 11:30 am and a group of twenty or so friendly folks had gathered from Illinois and several surrounding states to share in this rare occasion when the moon would totally eclipse the sun. The sky was clear blue with a few white puffy cumulus clouds lined up along the eastern and western horizons. Visitors were being introduced in small groups while others hurried to set up tripods with cameras or binoculars. Extra cardboard eclipse glasses were passed around in case someone had forgotten to bring a pair. Folding lawn chairs were set up in a freshly mown section of field between the hay barn and another out building where a 360 degree view of the noonday sky was unimpeded.

I had just finished setting up my 15 x 70 binoculars on a tripod so that the projected image could be viewed on a white sheet of paper showing the moon's transit across the face of the sun without looking through the lens directly, when someone shouted, *"First contact!"* The moon had just passed the right edge of the sun. Everyone began gazing sunward through their protective eclipse glasses. One fellow had a pair of binoculars designed for viewing solar eclipses and was looking directly at the sun. He offered them to anyone who might also want to take a look. A couple of folks were interested in my projection and moved the sheet of paper around in order to get the largest eclipse image into focus.

About the time the sun was two-thirds eclipsed, a large white, fluffy cloud scudded in from the East, obscuring the continuing eclipse at our location. Moans of despair erupted from many of the adult viewers. As folks fretted about the annoyance and possible termination of their eclipse viewing experience, the cloud seemed to be moving away from the sun.

To my amazement, I continued watching as the ambient light level seemed much brighter than I had expected, even with the sun more than half obscured. In fact, with approximately one=sixteenth of the sun's surface still visible, there seemed to be an extraordinary amount of light beaming toward earth. Within seconds, however, the light turned to twilight as if a gigantic dimmer switch in the sky had been suddenly turned down low.

There was a perceptible drop in temperature, the cicadas began their "sawing" chorus, the horses snorted and raced to the other end of their fenced enclosure, and Jupiter or Mars was visible in the western sky. The cloud lingered a bit longer causing our group of viewers to miss the first "diamond ring" and "Bailey's beads" as "second contact" occurred. But in a few moments the shroud of water vapor disappeared revealing "totality!"

Now was the time to view the spectacle through binoculars as the sun's glaringly hot surface was blocked completely from view by the moon – a black orb surrounded by solar flares and the sun's corona. Two minutes and 41.6 seconds later, "third contact" occurred. Eclipse glasses in hand, everyone anticipated the appearance of Bailey's beads, and the second diamond ring following close behind. Then the hidden light of the sun steadily returned to full brilliance and intensity, and needed to be viewed only through the protection provided by the special glasses.

Two couples had erected a tent canopy next to the old garage out-building to view some peculiar solar wind waves on a 3' x 4' white screen directed at the Sun. While looking at the concrete floor in the garage, I could see crescent shapes of sunlight that were beaming through holes in the old roof shingles, projecting onto the floor. What strange images.

After Bailey's beads and the trailing edge burst of the diamond ring, the light began slowly returning to full intensity. The cicada's quieted, the horses returned to grazing and drinking from a watering trough, the temperature elevated back to where it had been before the eclipse began, and the planet in the West disappeared. Most observers continued to watch in astonishment through their eclipse glasses, the rare astronomical spectacle that was about to come to a close until the next one can be viewed near this same location in 2024. It's predicted to be twice as long in duration -- over four minutes of "totality."

By 3:00 pm most of the solar eclipse watchers had expressed their "farewells" to the folks they had shared this momentous occasion with and began to depart. I moved my folding lawn chair beneath the shadiest tree I could find and endured the heat and humidity while sipping an ice-cold beverage. By f4:00 pm, the hosts arrived home from their professional duties at the university and invited all remaining visitors for a dip in their above ground pool. What a treat that was!

The water temperature must have been at least ten degrees cooler than the air temperature; the "cold" water was invigorating, actually raising goose bumps. The two young boys enjoyed frolicking in the water playing "Shark Attack!," while the adults traded observations about the day's events. After a long cooling-off soak, our hosts announced it was time to get ready for a special eclipse dinner at a local bar and grill. The sooner we could get there, the sooner we could eat.

We all changed back into our street clothes and then caravanned to the 17th Street Grill where hungry patrons were waiting in line for a vacant table. We waited patiently outside for most of an hour on picnic tables beneath a canopy with several other parties. To quench our collective thirsts, a round of 22-ounce bottles of the local brew, Big Muddy, was brought out to our table. Conversations shot in all directions, in English and in German, as complete strangers were introduced and friends made while waiting for an inside table. Finally, a table became available, orders were taken, and by 8:00 pm we were eating some of the tastiest barbecued ribs in all of southern Illinois (some would say: *all* of Illinois).

Mary chose to take the next day off and Mark drove the boys to school on his way to his office. Dean and I packed up our gear and loaded up the loaner ready for the trip back to the dealership and his repaired vehicle. We thanked Mary for the great time we had visiting their home and farm, in addition to all the wonderful memories that we shared. After filling the gas tank at $ 2.13 per gallon, we stopped for lunch and then began our drive back to Lansing, arriving just about midnight EST, August 22, 2017.

Pruning Apple Trees

The sky is overcast, making the late January sky look even colder. Temperatures are hovering between 25° and 30° F as I walk toward the silhouettes of bare-limbed apple trees. I've pruned the three apple trees on the church property for the past four years hoping to bring them back into production for use in the church's Fall Harvest Festival. Fresh, homemade applesauce or apple butter pairs well with roast pork loin and sauerkraut.

After the first pruning in January of 2014, a late spring frost nipped the trees as their blossoms set.

The following year the transparent variety produced a few apples, as did the two trees back in the corner, south of the garden. Two years ago the transparent tree produced a good number of apples that matured and dropped from the tree in early August. The two trees behind the garden produced the most abundant crop since being pruned, although the apples were unattractive due to blister rusts and other unsightly scabbing. Fortunately, the skins could be removed and the discolored portions of the apples pared away. Eight half pints of apple butter resulted from the efforts expended. A modest beginning.

Last year was another unproductive year after a late spring frost, producing only a few apples on the transparent tree and several high up in the other two.

Working with my pole saw, I begin thinning the canopy, removing branches whose twigs with summer leaves interfere with other branches and compete for sunlight. My yearly concern is the new "suckers" that grow vertically from the upper side of larger branches. These new shoots reach skyward to send another stem to display photon-catching green leaves to collect solar energy, providing nutrients for the tree (the process of photosynthesis).

The problem is that the growth of these shoots is expensive from an energy standpoint because they divert nutrients away from fruit and seed production. So, it's a trade-off to get a balanced approach to pruning each year. The overall goal is to have well-shaped trees with productive branches low to the ground, making harvesting available to hand-pickers without having to use a ladder.

As I went about my wintertime task, my stream of consciousness began to compare pruning an apple tree to the Biblical parable of pruning grape vines. I realized the similarities and how they relate to our individual lives. The useless, dead wood needs to be pruned and removed from the orchard or vineyard and burned, because it may host parasites or disease organisms that can spread to the good wood and fruit the following season. The untrained suckers need to be eliminated to keep the tree or vine engaged in producing fruit, not sapping energy for unbridled growth. Uncontrolled, causes the tree to grow taller and produce smaller fruit that is well out of easy reach for ease of harvesting. Some branches need to be eliminated because of their proximity to other branches and the resultant conflicts of shading and physical damage to maturing fruit caused by windy conditions during spring and summer thunderstorms.

Mid-winter is the best time of year to prune apple trees because of the dormancy caused by life-giving sap retreating to the root system. Loss of this vital life force while pruning is minimized when the sap is not flowing.

What better time than the early days of the New Year for us to take stock, as it were, of our own productivity and begin an annual "pruning" regimen. This exercise in re-directing the life force of the grape vine can apply to our own hearts and minds. We can strive to "prune" or eliminate unnecessary and often time-robbing activities and unhealthy behaviors that devour our limited energy and time.

These pastimes cause us to be less productive than we could, should, or otherwise would be in spreading the Good News of the Gospel to those within and to those without our circle of influence. After all, God blesses each of us with 168 hours of life each week (7 days times 24 hours each day) to live, breathe, work, rest, take care of ourselves and our families, and *bless* our Creator.

How many of us come near to tithing ten percent of our time each week to the maintenance of our Spiritual good health and that of our fellow congregants? Upon self-examination, I find there are certainly time-sapping "suckers" of my life that could be "pruned" away to provide more constructive time to study God's Word, praying, giving thanks, reaching out to those less fortunate, and joining in fellowship with other members of the church body.

We all need to be reminded that we enter *our* mission field as soon as we leave the comfortable confines of the physical church building.

-G.

James Link, January 23, 2018

Patricia Markham loves words; from sonnets to Scrabble games, from writing Bible Study curriculum to blog posts, from crossword puzzles to writing and illustrating children's books; she just loves words.

As an ordained minister, Pat has served alongside her husband as pastor, elder, and Bible teacher at Revival Center of Cadillac, Michigan since 1992. Her creative side is expressed in art, piano and of course - writing.

Since 1973 she as been married to the love of her life and produced a family of three sons and sixteen perfect grandchildren.

Beach Musing

It's worth the drive to nap down by the beach,
  And feel the gritty sand between my toes;
The rhythmic waves massage like soothing speech,
  'till tension ebbs out from my awkward woes.

I sketch and muse and dream of distant days
'neath geese in v-formation southward bound
And plot from here to there as through a maze;
A wishing I could hone my flight plan down.

Same wind that whips hair in my eyes below,
And chases ceaseless waves up to the shore;
  Lifts them aloft directing with its flow;
  Their destination unseen still, but sure.

  So in the Spirit's flow I will not strive
And at life's end I'll feel 'twas worth the drive.

Looking for Jesus

My Savior is no longer on that cross
Or limited by time and fleshly form.
Mortality for Him was not a loss.
Now moving through dimensions is His norm.

How can a finite mortal look for Him;
When natural eyes the spirit cannot see?
For He knows life beyond our bones and skin.
Yet comes the invitation, "Walk with me."

Mortality he folded with the shroud
And resurrection's first fruit he would be;
So I could be immortally endowed
The light of glory on His face to see.

To find that narrow entrance is the plight;
For now, I walk by faith and not by sight.

Untitled

So young was I when giving birth began;
Can children raising children comprehend
The fragile futures shaped in each mistake
Leaves grieving generations in their wake?

You hate me now, I know its true, and yet
You love me still, although with much regret.
Wound tight and bound with that maternal cord
Hate strangles while love gasps and grips its hold

Exhausted, drained and bruised, I can't go on
So on the altar I just lay us down
I've nothing left to give, no room to take
I pour them out like water love and hate

Forgive the past, both yours and mine, and heal
Fresh future plans and commons He'll reveal.

His Heart In Me

It softly comes while sitting at his feet;
The weight of glory soothing, still and deep.
Love's own agenda is what keeps me there;
Heart focused and engaged while lost in prayer.

To pray His passion moves His hand with speed.
But am I there? For sinners would I bleed?
Or pay love's steepest cost without regret?
I hear His words, but are they mine? Not yet.

Until His pulse and mine are one, I'll wait.
When sacrifice and cost lose the debate;
My motives based in selfishness all melt,
His tender heart toward vilest villain felt.

The love that held my Savior to the tree;
Will resurrect His heart to live in me.

The Winter of Lack

In the winter of lack the January Soul can choose to give in to grief over treasures and opportunities lost. Desperation strangles. Words of faith seem to die in the throat. The storm of questions blasts through the brain like a blizzard: Whose fault is this? Why me? Why now? Will it ever be right again? Where is God? Does He even care? The January Soul may slip down that icy slope into cold depression, "I'm frozen here - it's too late now - nothing will ever change." Yet when the January Soul chooses to resist the grief and blame, and to salt those icy slopes with thoughts and words of faith, the sliding stops and struggles cease. Faith invites the soul to come in out of the cold and rest by the fire.

"Come in from the cold. Come in to a new way of resting."

Waiting on God in the winter of lack is restful but not passive. We remain still to heal, to grow, to repair, to plan, to fix infrastructure, to lay new foundations, to correct positions and postures; the discipline of rest is a new kind of work. When the brain goes to sleep, the body relaxes and gets busy. When no conscious demands are being made on the body, the body does some of its finest work. Growing, repairing, rejuvenating, and purging - all happen in the uninhibited season of rest. January, even in a winter of lack, is an uninhibited season of rest for the January Soul. The winter of lack is time to sit by the fire and heal, and plan, and get right.

Warm yourself by the winter fire, and consider the lilies whose bulbs are resting beneath the ice crusted snow. They know that from their rest they are drawing the essence that without toiling or spinning on their part, will produce the finer than Solomon's array of splendor when their season is right. Take heart, January Soul, your winter of lack will give way to splendor for you also. Wait productively. Rest deeply. Have faith in God's immutable timing.

> *Luke 12:27: Consider the lilies, how they grow: they neither toil nor spin; and yet I say to you, even Solomon in all his glory was not arrayed like one of these.*

THE WINTER OF PLENTY
(Luke 12:16-21)

The ground of a certain January Soul had yielded plentifully in the harvest season, bringing him to the fateful choice of what to do with the "plenty". It couldn't have been wrong to enjoy the benefit of a job well done. It couldn't have been wrong to plan for the future.

So the January Soul asked himself, "What shall I do with what is mine; my crops, my barns, my goods?" How can I leverage what is in my hand to last longer and yield even more?"

Pity that he failed to see the "plenty" as a test. Instead he saw it as a reward for his labor and therefore his to do with or hoard as he saw fit.

The flawed assumption was that after God had created the ground and the seed, and provided the strength, wisdom, and understanding of agriculture for the January Soul, that God had also given that soul title to what was produced out of God's ground and God's seed. God had provided all the elements. The January Soul had only provided the labor: yet he assumed all was his to control without giving the Lord of the Land His due.

How differently this parable would have ended if the January Soul had said, "Let me rest in the presence of my Lord until He shows me His pleasure and gives me direction. Lord, everything that You have blessed and prospered in my hands I freely lay at Your feet as a sacrifice. Use it as You see fit. I trust You to care for me."

Then, God could have trusted that January Soul and began planning for a greater springtime investment of seed, richer summer soils, and more abundant harvests in the future.

In the Winter of Plenty there is at least the potential for the January Soul to become rich toward God. Recognize the test and choose wisely.

"Then he spoke a parable to them, saying, "The ground of a certain rich man yielded plentifully."

And he thought within himself, *What shall I do, since I have no room to store my crops?*

So he said, "I will do this. I will pull down my barn and build a greater one, and there I will store all my crops and my goods."

And I will say to my soul, "Soul, you have many goods laid up for many years; take your ease; eat, drink, and be merry."

But God said to him, "Fool! This night your soul will be required of you; then whose will those things be which you have provided?"

"So is he who lays up treasure for himself, and is not rich toward God" "

Ray Allen Smith lives in Okahumpka, Florida. Over his life he's trickled across the country, from North to South, West to East, across the ocean and back again, from factory to the Navy, airplanes to football, Fuller Brush man to graphic artist, mental hospital orderly to pharmacist, and finally, retiree to writer.

  He lives with his wife, Janet, and spends his time writing, golfing and enjoying his five children and nine grandchildren.

Not to Baltimore

There he was again, walking to work in his clean shirt and his pressed pants. She never missed his passing as he was always whistling. It seemed like he had a different tune each day. She could not name the tunes, for there was no music in her life. No music and no time. If she had been born a boy she could have done man's work, but as a found girl, she did housework and field work. No time for school or frivolities, so to her the whistled tunes were more precious than the whistler could ever imagine.

He knew she studied him. He did not have to study her. Everyone knew about her, the girl who acted like a man. Her overalls, her hair scrunched up under a railroad cap, her dirty face, not someone he needed or wanted to talk to. He was a found boy on his way up. His family chose him when the founding train stopped at Stoer's Junction. He had put the streets of Baltimore from his mind. No, no more rags for him, no more scrounging in the refuse for scraps, no more begging. He was stepping out. He was loved and cared for.

Came that cold morning, almost too cold to whistle. For sure the tune was lost in the wind. The wind that snatched his new hat as well and tumbled it across the field. Sent it dancing black against the snow. Sent it past the wrapped figure shoveling in the driveway.

She turned to stare at him as he galloped through the snow, first at her, then past her. She got a glimpse of bright teeth and a smile, gone too quick for her to smile back. The hat seemed to be circling, looking for an escape route. She dropped her shovel and joined the chase. The hat gained the barn-side and rolled on its brim, smooth and quick with a small hop every time she reached for it. He swore at the wind. She howled with laughter and with a burst of speed, cut the hat off, cracking the barn door open enough for it to pop in. She slipped in as well and caught it up, gripping it tightly as though it might escape again.

He stood in the darkened barn facing her. A few sunbeams danced thin spotlights where they could see their breaths meet and entangle. She had a scarf across her face.

"My hat," he said.

"So' tis. I'll be tradin' you for it."

He frowned not understanding the trade and confounded by the timbre of her voice. It brought to mind the tilt of a bluebird's head giving some small note, a note the caused one to turn an ear to the side waiting for the next.

They stood quietly until she unwound the scarf and shook her hair loose. "You up for a trade or can I keep the hat?"

That voice again, this time no need to dredge up pictures. The picture was before him. The flawless skin, the gently turned up nose, the sparkling green eyes, all framed in an impossible swirl of dark red hair, "Trade?" he croaked. A frog talking to a bluebird, "Trade for what?"

"I wish to know what you're whistlin'."

"Whistling?"

"Aye, whistlin'. You skip by here on school days whistlin' I don't know what. I'd like to know the names of those tunes."

"Why, 'Henry's Mule,' 'Turkey in the Straw,' 'Woodchoppers Hall' and such, you know, dance tunes."

"I do not know dance tunes and I cannot whistle."

"Can you sing?

"Never have. No one here sings and I have little to sing about."

"No one sings or dances? How old are you?"

"I am not certain. I was a found child from Baltimore,

but would guess I may be seventeen or so."

"A found child? I, too, am a found child. And now I've found you."

She smiled. A smile so full of wonder it surprised her. She felt it leap out from some hidden place within her. He felt it too and he matched it with one every bit as bright and warm. They stood there locked in place, face to face, until he leaned forward ever so slightly and she followed suit. Inch by inch their faces moved, riding on the light each could see in the other's eyes. The space was lost and their lips touched. Gently at first then firmer, their bodies followed, coupling up through layers of winter wear.

She was first to speak. "Never kissed nobody. Can't imagine ever kissing anybody else."

"No need to," he whispered in her ear. "I'll always be the one."

"How can you be so sure?"

He placed her hand inside his coat, over his heart. "Feel that?"

"I do."

"It beats only for you. We'll run off together. Will you go with me?"

"Oh, I will. Yes, I will."

"Tonight. Be here in this barn. I have money to buy Ephraim's horse. We will ride off into the night."

She kissed him again and asked, "Not to Baltimore?"

"No, not to Baltimore. To the moon and the stars, but never to Baltimore."

Outside the Box

The blankets draped over my arm warmed me and I held them close to my chest. A row of boxes lined the sidewalk where it crossed beneath the overpass. They offered little to the eye other than an evidence of urban blight. Yet, if analyzed, there was a certain neatness to the jumble. Different lengths, heights and depths belied an overall organization, but why be surprised. After all, they were inhabited.

I tapped gently on the first. No answer. Perhaps, no one home or no resident. Any other explanation I kept out of my head and moved on to the next box.

Tap, tap, tap again. This time a response came from the neighboring box. "He ain't there. Gone to the park to rouse up some cash money." The voice was graveled, a result of too much or too little. I moved to his long box. It was curtained on one end and the curtain was lifted. "What you need?" he asked.

"I'm good right now," I answered "but I've got some spare blankets here, thought maybe you could use one." A bent hand slipped out and I draped a blanket over it. In the dark slot behind the curtain I could see a pair of red-rimmed eyes.

"Obliged," he said, "see that red box?"

I turned my head. "I do."

"Young girl there. Needs a blanket for sure. Maybe more'n just a blanket."

I stood up and eyed the box. It appeared stouter than the other boxes, made of some light ply or stiff resin, maybe a shipping crate for a refrigerator. It was stained red and it stood alone, empty spaces on both sides of it. It, too, had a curtain and I could see a finger, with a chipped blue fingernail, holding it back.

A young girl? How young? And why? Troubled boys and destitute old men I could work with. But a young girl? I'd need some backup. I considered walking away, but I still had blankets and advice that might help. I squatted a few feet from her calico curtain.

"Hi there. My name's Don. I've got a couple of clean blankets here. Could you use one?"

The fingers moved forward and she lifted the curtain with her wrist. I was surprised to find her squatted like I was and our eyes met. Her face was smudged and a double line of dirt ran across one cheek. It was threaded with tear tracks. She'd been crying.

"Are you okay?" I asked

"Me? Never been better. The accommodations are less than perfect, but the view makes up for it."

"The view?" I was confused by the gentle lilt of her voice and the green of her eyes.

"Sure. I can see another row of boxes across the way, a real neighborhood. And when a train goes through, well, there's no telling what I might see. And speaking of surprises, you surely are one. You look nothing like my neighbors." She took a couple of duck walk steps and rose up.

I found myself looking up at her, held my poise for a minute and slowly stood up to face her. I am six-foot-three and look down on most women. This one met me almost eye to eye; she had to be all of six foot tall. "Blankets?" I couldn't think of anything else to say.

Now she added a smile; white teeth resting on a full lip. "Ah, yes, blankets. It tells me something, those blankets. Still it makes me wonder as to the why of it. Are you just plain good hearted? Could you be making amends for some past mistake? Have you ever been homeless?"

"Whoa, I have blankets. People get cold. I'm giving them blankets."

"Cryptic, but good enough. How about breakfast? Do you have that?"

This girl could eat. The breakfast bar had been a good choice. We hardly spoke as she went through scrambled eggs, bacon and flapjacks. She buttered a last biscuit and gave me an inquisitive stare. "We didn't share names."

"I gave you mine. What's yours?"

"Carlita."

"Just Carlita?"

"Yeah, just Carlita. Carlita and Don. Won't that do?"

"Yeah, it'll do. What now?"

"I shower at the Salvation Army. Want to go with me?"

"Well, I shower at home. You want to go with me? You can use my shower."

There was that smile again. "No funny business?"

I pushed myself away from the table. "No, no funny business. I'm a serious guy."

I could hear the shower running. I studied the newspaper and tried unsuccessfully to hold my imagination in check. Carlita carried no purse, only a small backpack and it was in the bathroom with her. She had been dressed in shorts and a L. L. Bean Tee-shirt. I offered her a clean Tee-shirt of her choice from my drawer. I waited to see which one she had chosen. I don't wait around for girls, but this one had me on a string and I didn't know why.

When she emerged tousling her dark hair with a towel I held out a coffee cup. Her shirt said: "Boomer Sooner," announcing my alma-mater, Oklahoma.

"Nice shirt," I said, "one of my favorites."

"Everything here is nice. I like this carpet and the leather furniture. Whoa, that is some big TV."

"A football indulgence. You likeTV?"

"Don't see much. Could we watch the news?"

"Which one? CNN, FOX, MSNBC?" I clicked the remote.

An hour passed with our feet on the ottoman and our noses in coffee cups.

"It's a mess isn't it? The world I mean."

"Yes, 'tis." I agreed.

"I'm a liberal. Are you liberal or conservative?"

"I like to think I'm conservative with a liberal bent."

She nodded. "You like to take care of others, but the country's going broke doing it."

I smiled at her, "And if we didn't waste so much, we could do more."

"And the fat cats get fatter."

"Yes, they do."

"Don't you go to work?"

"Not today, today is my day off. I have one day off and I spend it, or at least part of it doing what I did this morning."

She got up and walked to the window staring out at the rooftops and blue sky.

"What are you thinking?" I asked.

She looked over her shoulder at me and raised one eyebrow. "I'm wondering why anyone would work six day a week. Do you like what you do at work better that what you do on your day off?"

"No, no I don't. In fact I don't like my job all that much. I'd like to find something else."

She smiled the smile I found myself waiting for whenever she spoke. I felt a gentle tension while waiting for her next sound and move. I was cataloguing them, and when she stretched and rolled her neck in a circle, I stopped breathing for a few seconds.

"What about lunch?" she asked. "First Baptist serves a good one."

Now I was smiling. "Do you like salmon? I have salmon and the makings of a salad."

She put a long finger on my nose then drew a line down my cheek and along my jaw. "How about we do it together?"

We stood at the sink. She was washing and I was drying. I felt her eyes on me and turned toward her. She put a wet hand on my shoulder and kissed me softly. "You are a sweet man," she said in a soft voice. She pulled the dishtowel from my hands and used it to dry her own.

I watched her walk across the room and pick up her backpack. "You're leaving?" I asked.

"Taking a walk. I always walk after lunch. You coming?"

The park was quiet: a mother pushing a stroller, two old men on a bench, and a young boy trying to teach a puppy to fetch. We walked awhile and stopped to laugh at the puppy. I looked down and we were holding hands.

"I suppose its time," she said.

"Time?"

"Time to go home."

"You can stay at my place. Come home with me."

"I already have." Her eyes were wide as she stared into mine. "You could come home with me."

"Home with you? But you live in a box."

"I do. And you have to go to work tomorrow." Her hand slipped from mine, and I watched her walk away.

To Michigan author and artist **Carolyn Tody,** good stories celebrate the irrepressible energy of our human spirit and our search to reinvent and balance and explore the underpinnings of life. Besides developing characters and globetrotting, she combines numerous creative callings with her personal gallery of mixed media art to illustrate some of the stories and poems that appear in roughly twenty print and online collections. Ask her sometime about the invitation from a media giant that convinced her to publicly share her stories.

Carolyn received her degree from Michigan State University. She is career veteran of over a hundred professional management skills development workshops, including Disney University, and has a diverse set of certifications. Currently, she lives in Lansing with her amazing grown children. She enjoys connecting with readers wherever you are: www.facebook.com/Carolyn.Tody.Author, **www.amazon.com/author/carolyntody**, and her new website, www.artfulcharm.com.

Evolutionary Change

Carolyn Tody

Change is a condition on which the world turns
Fueling winds that blow steady and strong
Modifying our approach to a mortal existence
Electrifying old pathways we journey along.

As youngsters and teens we contemplate

How life begins and what eternity means
Moving into our teens and twenties and thirties

Love is the currency for elusive life dreams.

Soon our backs hew the wall of weighty goals

We cannot give up on decisions we have made

So we cringe, move ahead then wait, for what?

Confronting change becomes a challenging grade.

Commitment is the key to our fifties and sixties

We transmute **anyway** into power **'any'** way

Our high paced lives conceal speeding hours

Rendering us blind to the time that passes astray.

Time is a great transformer of abstract ideas

As modern pace conceals the hours speeding by

And as the world spins on people toil and play
With scant understanding of wherefore and why.

At six decades and seven and upward and onward
The tempo of change spirals past with a flash

Revealing that our lives are quickly departing
Our eighties and nineties hit with a mighty crash.

When humanity grasps that truth so existential
Temporal life springs into a swift, swirling flame
Wise humans would adapt a life changing action

We adjust how we play the rules of Life's Game.

The evolutionary forces of wind, water, and time

…Yield a human chronology of change sublime.

Guardian
Carolyn Tody

Freezing rain was drizzling down
    When I nearly earned my angel crown
While I lightly touched the auto brake
    Outside my spinning car pounced Fate.

The vehicle spun right; over stumps we flew
    Doors tore clean off and ejected us two
Difficult, witnessing all of our idols fall
    Humans are only mortals barely able to crawl.

My tires were spinning; my hair was a mess
    A huge male passenger lay across my chest
Trees to every side left naught for error
    How could we have survived this rainy lair?

My invincible guardian angel is now at rest
    What special purpose deserves his bequest?
What unique new world is my task to create?
    …I will inspire new life dreams that radiate.

Tristan

When she first saw him, Lorelei was driving on a dirt road in light rain that threatened to freeze. A full moon was rising. Its golden luminescence shone through the uppermost branches of treetops, washing the sky with an amber glow like distant lamplight, backlighting his dark hair.

She sighed… and lightly touched her brakes.

Her car launched and became airborne; it turned right ninety degrees, flew across a ditch, tore off her driver side door, and catapulted her through headfirst into a dense wood.

~

For untold seconds Lorelei lay there, stunned, wondering if she was even alive. When she did move, it was with a groan. The world hung upside down. She felt no pain, but during those first few precious moments, the trees surrounding her were all that made sense.

Her returning memory brought a rush of apprehension. When she lifted her eyes to the dark blue sedan, she cried tears of pure disbelief to see its tires still spinning, because its undercarriage was suspended on newly cut tree stumps that rose only in that part of the ditch.

She was alive. There was no refuting the physical evidence. A severed steel door protected her belly from sharp branches and wet earth underneath. Tall trees grew in a dense formation around her tiny space. She touched one. Its bark felt solid, almost rigid, and extremely real. Yet she was certain no one could survive such an impossible situation. The odds against missing a tree were too great. She wanted to lie there forever and turn back the hands of time until she had one more go at deciding whether or not to drive today.

Lorelei roused enough to realize she could not linger in the cold mist. Someone needed to fetch help. She tested her legs. They seemed intact, so she clutched a fallen branch and raised herself onto unsteady feet. From there she limped to the car. Its floor was above her head and she could do nothing to drag it from the stumps. She was too disoriented to conceive of finding help on the deserted dirt road, so she lurched through the woods, bewildered and bedraggled, hoping to find help somewhere in the remote countryside.

Only then did she spot him again through the trees. She wanted to ask him for help. Instead she paused, hesitant to approach the hilltop where he stood. His silhouette fell against a passing cloud, where he appeared to be watching the sky transform from liquid denim to starlight. This terrified her. It was nearly impossible to tell when night would descend and trap her alone in the darkness with him. Even so, she moved closer until she had his profile sandwiched against the moon. She was positive he'd been watching her watch him earlier.

Tristan rose, and began to glide smoothly across the uneven ground as if he was floating. The swollen tops of meadow grasses brushed pollen across his long hair.

From this distance, Lorelei saw only his black hair backlit by the moon. A sudden breeze shifted his billowing shirt and revealed the chiseled lines of finely tuned chest muscles underneath.

Tristan shivered, knowing she was close. He had realized the road surface was close to freezing, had tried to tell her not to spin out on the ice. He was too far away to help. All he could do was watch her rise and walk away in confusion. Just then, a swarm of tiny fireflies lit his face. To them he whispered, "Go to her, lazy little stars," to those that lit on the palm of his hand.

Lorelei saw the halo of tiny, bursting, iridescent lights sparkle around his head in the twilight, making it look as if he wore a fiery crown of ghost light. Watching him watch her from behind his hand washed away her confusion. He warmed her soul. She watched, but he seemed to pose no threat, and she stepped closer. The fireflies surrounded her hair with their glow.

Taking care not to spook her, Tristan paused to inhale the aroma of young saplings, trying to breathe in their perfume until his soul expanded and saturated her with deep feeling. "Moonlight," he whispered softly, bowing his head so she did not hear his words, "carry this scent to her."

Lorelei froze. It was more than the shock of the accident. Something impaled her heart. She imagined floating in the sweet incense of night blooming perfume. Indeed, a thousand fragrances scented the air. Some were as subtle as a whiff of Jasmine; others were spicy, or minty, or rich with musky intoxication. She wondered if she would ever return to this magical place, where she expanded larger than life into all that was or ever would be. Her shocked senses wanted the timeless moment to carry her into eternity, feeling as one with him and the heavens.

As the two stood watching each other, the moon crested the treetops and their shadows cascaded over the meadow.

"We are in darkness," whispered Tristan, louder this time, "yet under the moon we cast a misty vagueness of light." He raised his face to meet her gaze.

Lorelei locked her hungry eyes on his with undeniable yearning. Lorelei had never seen anyone so enigmatic, so mysterious.

Finally, Tristan walked slowly into her embrace, knowing that neither of them would find another grail in their endless universe of striving. He was hers, and she was his. For the better part of an hour they stood together, locked in intense embrace, both mysterious, neither willing to relinquish the spell that bound them.

Wild creatures rarely stay the same for long. When the moon rose higher, Lorelei sensed a movement at the edge of the woods. Her concentration was broken. She tore her eyes from Tristan, startled to see a fawn emerge. But when she turned back Tristan was gone. The night had swallowed him.

Tristan watched her from the darkened forest some distance away; he searched uncomprehendingly for the men who caused his distress. He knew they were near.

At that moment, a red clad pheasant hunter appeared from the opposite trees. His canvas pack bulged; he carried a shotgun level ahead as if he didn't know what to expect. A second shooter in blaze orange followed him into the moonlit clearing.

Whey they saw Lorelei in the meadow, swooning and bleeding from a head wound, they immediately dropped their gear and raced to her.

"You alright, Miss?" said the hunter in red.

Lorelei seemed genuinely puzzled to see the men.

The hunter wearing orange grasped Lorelei's hands and spread his coat for her to sit. When she was comfortable, he said, "Are you in pain, young lady?"

Lorelei shook her head. She was still not making sense of everything that had happened.

The red clad hunter fished a phone from his bag and dialed 911. "We need help here!" he shouted. "Make it quick, will you? We have a young woman bleeding out here, and it's raining." He listened briefly, and said, "Yes, conscious. Dazed. What? There was an accident... two miles south of Nichols. We spotted wreckage near the road and searched the fields." He jiggled the phone. "Can't hear you. Oh, the name's Brent Thomas. How long? Okay," he said, and disconnected. "They'll be here in fifteen minutes. Ron, can you get her a blanket from the car?"

"Sure thing," said Ron. He left and returned minutes later with a soft green wool coverlet.

Brent wrapped the blanket around Lorelei. She shuddered, so he sat beside her until she was warm. Then he said, "You made quite an impact on those trees."

Lorelei nodded. She scanned the tree line for Tristan, but saw nothing.

Brent gestured toward the road. "Ron is warming our vehicle. Can you walk? We need to flag someone down, and your car is impaled so you'd better wait where it's warm." He took the stunned young woman's hand and led her gently toward the road.

Lorelei did not protest. She was cold, and wet, and confused; but one day she would return to look for the mysterious black haired man with intense amber eyes.

Tristan saw that she was safe and stepped into the mist, realizing there was no better ending for a man who had just experienced perfect bliss.

The Old Storyteller
by Carolyn Tody

    Gitchi arises before dawn and retrieves a pair of worn moccasins left beside a waterfall. She ambles past an old wooden lodge. Every swish of her long skirt sends her thick braid swaying, as if it is a metronome moving to the beat of her worried mind and any moment the pace of modern change will threaten to swallow those she loves the most, as if she dare not wait.

    The elderly storyteller strolls south. She crosses the Leland River Bridge, and turns onto a lane heading west of town toward majestic Lake Michigan. There is no better place than the beach, with its view of the Manitou Islands, to search her soul for a parable dealing with change. Later this afternoon she will tell the story to tribal children.

    She eases herself through a narrow passage between the bushes lining the beach and swats away an insect swarm resembling finely ground black pepper. Her leather-clad feet slide down a sandy dune. Almost immediately, a great sapphire harbor bursts into view. She drops her sandy moccasins beside a sand castle that children have built to protect a delicate clamshell stranded among the dune grass in case its occupant returns. The gentle breeze is refreshing. Her bare toes burrow into the wet sand, and she feels that familiar connection to Mother Earth. A great smile spreads across her face. For several minutes she sits cross-legged on the cool sand listening to the musical sound of waves. Then she rises and walks on, collecting driftwood that floated in on a morning wave.

    This ancient beach has long provided her with sanctuary. She enjoys the pulsing lake with its captivating colors. It is only here at the water's edge, that she can calmly confront her fear about changes taking place in the Village of Leland which visitors lovingly dub "Fishtown."

What was it the elders said about passion when she was young? "Tame your passion and you will find your patience." Ahh, an insight flashes through her senses. It is *patience* she seeks here… patience to quit spinning her wheels in the past and deal with the rapid change propelling her family into the future.

"Great Mother," she says, "Lake Michigan is my passion, but how can Brother Michi Gami teach me patience?" Gitchi raises her arms to the wind and stands there waiting for her answer. The reply arrives so quickly that she wonders why she hasn't always understood. Wind and waves rushing across Brother Lake calm her restlessness at the same time they fuel her passion. Should she tell the children a story about wind, or is there something special about the water that energizes the wind?

"Great Mother, thank you for your gifts," she says, "and for the grace to carry out my charge as storyteller. But, Earth Mother, how can the wind and waves help me speak to the children about finding peace in the midst of change?"

Gitchi needs to find the right tale, because story time later this afternoon is an opportunity to pass elder wisdom to youths who gather at the tribal fire. She faces the Manitou Islands with her toes barely above the wave line, inhales the fresh lake air, and attempts to reconcile fear about her own son's future. A glance across the shining expanse of water reminds her of the Ojibwe legend about Mishe Mokwa and her cubs:

The twin cubs sought to escape a great forest fire on the Wisconsin shore. Mishe Mokwa swam with them across Lake Michigan, toward the Michigan shoreline. Eventually the cubs tired, fell behind, and drowned. Mother Bear paced the Michigan shore waiting for her babies. Great Spirit understood her grief and covered the cubs with sand to form the Manitou Islands; and then, extended a sleeping spell over Mishe Mokwa so that she lay underneath the northern Michigan sand dunes, forever facing the islands that cover the bones of her cubs.

Gitchi turns back to the deserted stretch of beach. "Great Mother, I too have a story. I fear my son will drown like the cubs, trying to swim against the current of changing times. Will he adapt? Will he prevail? Or am I like the Mother Bear, forever lying on the beach, waiting for my children to make it to shore? How do I resolve my fear? How do I draw from my saddened heart a new story with sensible native principles to guide the children?"

For the next hour, the old woman trudges along the Lake Michigan shoreline while the rising sun dazzles the world with energy. She stoops, admires a spider web spun the night before. She observes the sparkle of sunshine reflecting off water around the islands, and scowls at distant clouds casting their shadows upon the lake. Eventually she pauses to reminisce about how time has changed her life.

"Great Mother," she says. "many years ago, my family fished with nets. A new law stopped the tribe from using them, and tribal restitution gave my husband the funds he needed to start his own great lakes fishing charter. He prospered even further with the new Chinook and Coho salmon sport fishery. Later, my son Paul took over the profitable business, but he suffered when fishermen purchased their own luxury boats equipped with the latest technology. Paul changed with the times. He outfitted canoes and kayaks, but the sale of cheaper versions enabled people to fish the rivers on their own, and his business dwindled. What will he do now?"

Gitchi walks on, her heart aching with longing for the time when her people earned their livelihood with nets. The red glow of dawn gives way to swiftly moving clouds. She feels a sudden change in the air. Quicker than she can react, the wind rises and whips her long braid.

Dark clouds gather; they roll inland, driving currents of rain across the sky. Crashing waves beat the shore. Wind sandblasts the distant beach walkers with a fitful force that is gusty at times, assaultive at others. She races for shelter among the trees, with huge drops pelting the sand behind her.

The storm wages its war upon those below who fear change. Lake Michigan roils, smashing waves against one another in a frenzy of whitecaps.

The old woman imagines fish diving further into its depths. She pulls her own head deeper behind the thrashing pine branches.

This tempest finally sweeps inland across the Leelanau Peninsula in its haste to reach the great bay beyond. The great lake moans like a primordial beast healing a mortal wound. Sunshine sneaks out between the thunderclouds, casts its eerie glow upon the waves, and lulls fish into once again lifting their heads.

This time, Gitchi keeps an eye on the clouds as she ventures out from protective trees. She retraces her steps along the beach, allowing the sun to dry her wet clothes. She retrieves her moccasins and driftwood from puddles of water that appear where her footprints dented dry sand only moments before.

Once again, she reaches the narrow opening in the bushes, where damp weather has awakened more flies. She swings the driftwood at a swarm flying at her. This time, the black insets do not merely converge on her feet; they turn aggressive and engulf her face in black orgy clouds.

Gitchi wills her worn moccasins to carry her feet swiftly over the bridge. She races toward a battered wooden shack in Fishtown, where fishermen once repaired their nets, and rushes inside to stand beside its one small window. A swirling black haze swats the glass. She waits for the flies to leave. A quick glance out the window makes her realize how much the quaint little fishing village has changed since a hundred years ago, when summer guests arrived on the first passenger steamer from Chicago, although some of the faded, weather-beaten shanties are still used for eateries and shops. Finally, she understands. Life adapts and goes on.

The old storyteller brings closure to her meditation. "Now I know what to tell the children about change, Great Mother. Each of us, even the black fly, has a story that is part of a greater narrative moving us toward the coming times. At the same time, all we have is the present moment, reinventing itself, second by second, to meet the challenge of survival. Our children must learn to dance in the storm while they evolve toward their future."

Soon the tribal fishermen return from a day on the great lake. They light a small bonfire that drives away insects along a stretch of beach by the fishing shanties. Tribal children spot the flames and race in from every direction.

Gitchi emerges from the shack. "Relax, children," she says. "There's enough room for everyone." Milling, shoving youngsters part to let her sit on a high stump where everyone can hear and she can dangle her feet toward the fire as evening falls. "How many of you saw that storm pass through earlier today?"

Only a handful of chattering youngsters raise their hands before she begins her address. "Today the story is about a storm called Scout, a wave named Amber, and a little shell known as Curve."

Immediately the children hush, realizing a story is underway, and the storyteller begins.

"Amber the Wave is calm and lazy and forever sighing, 'I love to sparkle in the sun.'

"But whenever Scout the Storm visits the great lake, he blows and blows. Between bolts of lightning, he

screams, 'Crash about, you waves! Toss sand around the trees. Alter the landscape. You must create change.'

"Amber the Wave sees Scout coming. 'Get away from me!' She shouts. She tries to flatten her swells, but Scout's wind crashes into Amber and sweeps her into the beach along with water-borne seeds, to grow new and different plants in puddles that now litter the sand, and a fresh load of sand, shells and driftwood."

Gitchi raises the wet, broken pieces of driftwood she's collected on the beach to show the children; they cheer and she resumes her story.

"Oh, nooo," cries Curve the Shell, the first time Amber the Wave crashes down on her. The storm overwhelms her. Every time that Curve resists the wave, Amber knocks the little shell over and tumbles her around so she can't fill her air chambers and float back to shore.

"Eventually, though, Curve grows tired of resisting the wave. Amber sweeps her into the lake along with the scattered grains of her ruined sandcastle. Gradually, Curve figures out how to survive these many visits from Scout and Amber by diving into the wave and coming up for air until Amber relaxes. Then she swims out the other side and back to land. She suns herself on the beach waiting for the children to return and build her a new sandcastle.

"Scout flies above them, so high in the sky that he can see what is still far away - perhaps even into the distant future. He returns often to keep Amber and Curve in motion. Together their partnership moves the shoreline forward toward a secret dream that nobody understands except the elements."

"You see," says the storyteller, "Scout sends Amber to wash away the annoying debris that gets in the way of whatever Curve most desires."

"Does Curve ever get what she wants?" asks a child in a dark pigtail that is a miniature version of Gitchi's own braid. "Do her dreams come true?"

"Her dreams do come true," says Gitchi, "because all of life is one long change and Curve adjusts to the changing times. She learns to weather the storms that enter her life, and…"

Gitchi pauses. How clearly she sees it all now. The only real failure in life is refusing to try. Good things were occurring today, even after the storm has thrown her into a swarm of black flies. Nature is ending her need for life to remain the same. Lake Michigan is teaching her how to celebrate change. What's more, her time alone in the cedar shack is enabling her to glimpse the future.

The Ojibwe Elder is learning the value of weathering change while doing the best she can with today. Paul's business will continue. Her son will survive the current storm of competitive technology, and adapt to changing times as well as he can.

"…and the only thing that Scout, and Amber, and Curve - or you, my children, can ever know about the future," smiles the old storyteller, pausing to look into each little face, "is that the future will be different from today."

I, **Bette Waller**, was born and spent my childhood in Louisiana then moved to Dallas, Texas during my high school years. I began college in Fort Worth, Texas at Texas Christian University. Due to my mother's illness, I ended up leaving TCU after two years. I moved home to watch over her and complete the last two years of college in Dallas. I graduated from Southern Methodist University.

I began teaching in New Orleans, Louisiana and later moved to Killeen, Texas, teaching on the Fort Hood Military Base.

I married my husband, who was from Michigan and stationed at Fort Hood. We moved to Lake City, Michigan in 1996. We have five children and eight grandchildren.

I've carried the same enjoyments of life with me since childhood. I love traveling to other states and countries, learning how people live and writing about people and places in my journals. I love reading, especially history and historical fiction, with soft background of classic music.

I finally picked up writing more than pages in journals due to Write to Publish, (WTP). This has been a great way to review places visited and people to whom I've been drawn.

Northern Michigan is a well kept secret of beauty with four well-defined seasons. Since moving to Michigan I've added the pleasure of studying the animal wildlife around us and meeting new friends who share my love of writing also.

The Faces of Fear

    If there is one thing I've learned in all the years since my war, it is that certain sounds push me back into that period of time I so want to forget. It's raining, and this is the third day of rain. Rain. Mud. The sound of the wind picks up and the hard driving rain is more like bullets hitting the side of the house. It's been fifty years. Why can't I just forget?

    Sitting down on the side of the bed, holding my aching head between my hands, I wish I could turn a switch and the flash backs would stop. It's the rain that makes the flashbacks so vivid. Sometimes it's a plane flying low, or sitting around a bonfire…whatever. When shadows unfold at dusk, I can see the tall grass fields we moved silently through hoping the sound of our steps wouldn't alert the Cong to where we were or in which direction we moved.

Already my stomach is churning as anxiety begins to rise with the memories. The full force of fear will soon follow. The ending of these vivid replays is always the same: migraine headaches leading to cold sweats and nausea. The fearful thoughts and feelings have surfaced less and less as the years have gone by, but they still return one to two times a year ending with sleepless nights and the loss of a day or two of work.

    This time, I'll force myself to stay with the fear and work through the days I spent over there. I'll keep the mental pictures flowing and follow the trail from the beginning of fear all the way to the end, and perhaps, finally be done with it. I'll take it from day one to the day I hopped off a Trans-World airplane in California when I returned to the good ole USA. Pulling my chair over to the window and watching the rain pour down on my side of the world while I thought back all the way to the beginning.

It was only two weeks after graduation from high school when the Government letter arrived. It began, "Greetings." I read the rest in disbelief. After all, I had just put on my nicest shirt to go job hunting. Being out of school was sure full of surprises, I mused, and discarded my plans for today. Grabbing the letter and yelling to mom that I would be back in a couple of hours. I headed out to the recruitment center in Lansing, Michigan.

The next months were a blur of goodbyes, basic training at Fort Knox, onto South Carolina for individual Advance Technical Training. And then this was followed by a ride on a C130 heading to Vietnam.

"Shoot," I said to my seat-mate, as we tried to settle-in for the long haul to a war halfway around the world. "I don't even know where Vietnam is. I knew there was a war, but I've been busy with schoolwork and graduation. I haven't had time for this war or politics. Now I'm part of it. Lord, how did I get here?"

Sleep finally arrived. All sixty of the men aboard the flight slept and had full meal before landing at an airport near Saigon.

When the cabin door opened the sergeant stood and quickly ordered, "Get off this plane as fast as possible, duck your heads low and run to the pavilion in front of you. Your commander will meet you inside. We're taking fire and I want to get airborne again as quick as possible ....GO!"

Stairs had been moved to the opening and we began to file out. I heard gunfire followed by the sounds of bullets hitting the side of the plane.

Someone behind me yelled, "I don't think we're in Kansas anymore."

I didn't turn around. Now the sound of a machine gun caught my attention. I ran faster than I had ever run before, through a rain storm that poured so hard I could barely see the pavilion ahead.

As a commander spoke to us about our "next step," my eyes caught sight of a poster behind him. It read, "Welcome to Vietnam." Were they kidding?

Anxiety built as we boarded several "Duce and a Half," canvas covered trucks. Halfway to our final stop, we got out and lined up to receive rifles and bands of ammunition. Someone said this was Cu Chi and the GIs based here were called Wolfhounds.

Dau Tieng was a bit farther north and supposed to be a fairly safe basecamp. It was home to the 25th Infantry, which I was about join. There wasn't much time to get used to the hut, containing my cot and foot locker.

Life here quickly became a series of patrols. On the day patrols there were 20-25 of us. We visited villages and kept tabs on how far away the VietCong were, and sometimes routed them out of the villages. We also tried to help the people there. I didn't mind the day patrols as much as the night ones. At night there were only 3-6 men.

We were to stay hidden, not to engage anyone in, "No Man's Land," but rather listen and stay alert for enemy groups. We were to report anything of interest by radio. Base wanted to know if it were a company of Viet Cong or an enemy night patrol and in which direction they were moving. If we couldn't avoid contact, we were to silence them as quickly as possible.

"Wish we could get a transfer." Carl's closest friend, Mike began. "I can't stand this! All I do when we get back to camp is wonder when we'll be sent out again."

For the most part I was with the same three guys on night patrols. Mike, Andy and me knew in what position each was best and we had learned to move as one. We leaned one another. We knew each other's capabilities. All three of us were strong and understood what to do when. We must have been good on night patrols as we appeared to get sent out more than others. And, every time we stepped into "No Man's Land" anxiety and fear rose higher and lasted longer.

It was October and the monsoon period had just begun. The rain soaked us, kept our human sounds down and allowed us to cover ourselves in mud, blending in with the night. I'll never forget the mud. Our boots would sink all the way up to the laces. It made a sucking noise as we raised a foot to take another step. Sometimes, I can still hear it.

A couple of days after ole Mike made his wish to stop the patrols we were told they had a new mission for us.

"You'll join a group leaving by helicopter this afternoon. Don't worry, "Puff the Magic Dragon" with its super firepower will be flying in front. You'll be dropped in an area to help support Special Forces in holding the top of Black Virgin Mountain."

Puff not only sprayed bullets down on the enemy from the front, but he had powerful machine guns on each side. Mike, Andy and I were in the second copter called a Huey. We were sort of crammed in the middle along with six others. The third copter was a "Huey" also. We were dropped near the top of what I call a large hill. It wasn't a mountain to me; just a big hill. The rain had stopped for a little while and everything was quiet.

It didn't take any of us long to realize the importance of this place. There were two towers one could climb and see forever. Easy to spot troop movement and size. I let Mike and Andy know I could spend the rest of my tour here. It felt so safe.

Before nightfall, the Captain with Special Forces gave those of us from the 25th a briefing. We were anxious to know why we were here.

"Step this way," the Captain said, " I want to show you something we discovered late in the day during the last battle here."

He walked us over to a little tree, reached down and raised a hidden door which lifted the tree along with the ground around it, exposing a tunnel going down at an angle and through the hill.

"The reason you are needed is our "safe" mountain, as you called it, is on top of several tunnels and caves. We lowered a man into one of their tunnels. He told us they had a passage so wide that two trucks could pass each other side by side. When the Viet Cong decide they want to take this lookout back, they'll come up from the tunnels and be all over the place. We need help in marking each tunnel and destroying as many as possible. Night is coming. Stay alert."

It was on Black Virgin Mountain that the cold sweats began. It seemed with each passing hour something new developed to go with the sweats. Nausea and cramps appeared. I prayed for God to send helicopters to take us away from here.

The first night was fairly quiet. From our hilltop we spotted VietCong troop movement and called in the coordinates. We watched as our bombers did their job. When the skies cleared there was no sign of movement anywhere as far as the eye could see on every side.

The next night we learned what "stay alert" meant on Black Virgin Mountain. They came out of the tunnels and from every side. In the dark of night, we ran, fought, hid, tripped, slid, shot, and died. Within a couple hours they began to disappear. At least those who could run away did. Our side declared victory. But what about the nights to come? This was not a safe place.

The 25th's camp wasn't either. Both were hit hard the same night. Both battles were won by our side but carried heavy losses. When we returned to the 25th we discovered our friendly Vietnamese barber had been killed. That kind barber, who cut my hair, was a member of the VietCong. No one is safe anywhere in this country. An attack could come at anytime, or at any place. I ached to go home.

That night, overcome with weariness, I started to climb into my sleeping bag. Just in time I remembered the warning about snakes and did what we were taught to do. I unzipped the bag and opened it. Coiled inside was a black snake we called the "Two-Stepper." One bite and a person would take about two steps before dying. I lifted the bag carrying it outside our hut and shook the snake out onto the ground before killing it.

Tears I couldn't stop began to trickle down my face. I wanted to throw my gun and knives away... to listen to music... go to the drugstore for a coke... eat dinner with my family. I wanted to be where cars run up and down the streets, and people walking together are laughing and talking. I want freedom to go to church, to believe in my fellow man and to live. My thoughts ran wild that night. If only I could get home...if only...I started trembling and shaking with silent sobs. Death seemed to be everywhere.

"Carl, I'm home," Sandy called, smiling as she entered the room. "Lets go out on the porch and enjoy the rain."

As she took my hand the dark memories began to recede. I had known the highest level of fear during my year in Vietnam. Now, I live in peace. The war of long ago is beginning to fade back into the distant past once again.

I still don't understand that war. It didn't seem to solve anything. I don't know the why of it, or even what we were supposed to accomplish in the long run. Maybe there are many like me who wonder why we ever got involved over there. Why this heavy load of horror was grafted into our lives?

My prayer is for the One who brought me home to

fill me with thankfulness and keep the dark forces of the world away. Not to allow yesterdays to overshadow the love and joy of life we share in the here and now.

Mike, Andy and I truly know what it means to have been given the gift of life; to be brought home again, to pick up the pieces, put them all in the proper places and to work spreading peace, love and prayers for our fellowman in all areas of this world.

I smiled at Sandy as we sat listening to the gently falling rain. It was a rain that blesses the spring flowers. And, it was a rain that washed away memories of fears which no longer served any purpose.

Royalty in the Classroom

Aaliyah walked into my Third Grade classroom alone on the first day of school. No mama needed here to hold a hand and calm fears. She was a regal beauty in command of it all. Head held erect atop a long, elegant neck, she glided into our lives with posture as perfect as that of a ballerina. Her eyes swept the room, taking in everything. I got the feeling of slow motion when she surveyed me, the desks and all the children who had arrived before her. Slowly, she floated to a desk in the back of the room ad sat down as gracefully as any twenty year old model. This was going to be one interesting year.

The bell rang and I stood up to welcome the children to the Third Grade. "I'm Mrs. Gravett and will be your teacher this year. It's delightful to see bright faces on students ready to learn new things and have lots of fun doing so."

Just as I was about to talk about places and skills we would be working on during the year, Aaliyah's hand went up. "Yes, Aaliyah."

She stood slowly as everyone turned to see who was talking. "Mrs. Gravett, will we be studying other countries?"

"This is the year for a good bit of American history, Aaliyah, but if there is a certain country you would like for us to study, I believe it can be arranged."

"Yes, thank you. I would like to study Egypt. I am Egyptian."

"Well, I'm from Alabama." Billy chimed in.

Sally said she was from Washington. Another yelled out, "New York," and the room was quickly turned into a shouting match of where everyone was from. We were a school on a huge military base. Almost everyone was from somewhere else.

"Class, please raise your hand to be called on to speak. What the new student is sharing is that her family is from another country, Egypt. Were you born here in the United States or in Egypt, Aaliyah?"

"I was born in Egypt." Aaliyah said softly. "I'll explain more when the time is right."

When the time is right, I thought. My, she has all my curiosity building now. The rest of the day went well. We talked about our hopes for the coming school year. Aaliyah didn't enter into the conversations, but listened with a remarkable surreal expression on her face. I saw several children at different times turn to look at the little girl who was Egyptian.

Time moved quickly and finally we were drawing the end of the first school day. "It's my custom to have a Community Circle at the end of each week. This is only day one, but I believe it well help us get to know each other. How about everyone going to the open space at the back of the classroom and sit down on the carpet in a circle?"

Children made their noisy way to the back of the room and I waited until all were seated. Picking up a little ball, I began walking to the back of the room while giving the rules of the Community Circle.

"I'm holding the ball that gives a student the right to speak. After I tell you something about myself, I'm going to toss the ball to someone else. That person will then tell something about themselves, their family or how they feel about getting back to school."

I took a chair and pulled it into their cross-legged circle. "Ok? I'm Mrs. Gravett. I'm from the state of Louisiana and began teaching seven years ago. My husband and I are both in the education field. He's an administrator for our high school and we have a little girl who is six years old."

With that I threw the ball to Jim.

"I'm Jim Stevens. I like baseball and played baseball all summer." Jim threw the ball to another classmate.

"I'm Linda Gaston. My family went to Washington, DC this summer."

And so, the "getting to know you" circle continued until finally the ball was thrown to Aaliyah. She caught the ball and quietly set it in her lap looking down for a moment. As she raised her head, she swept the circle with large brown eyes, and began to speak softly.

"My name is Aaliyah Anippe. Aaliyah means "Daughter of the Nile." My family came to America and to this military base because of my father. We will be here for a few months."

She stopped speaking while her eyes made another sweep of the circle. With her voice growing ever stronger, she said, "I am going to tell you a secret that we have not told anyone here yet."

This time there was lengthy pause. "I am an Egyptian princess. It is difficult not speaking about this to others, but I want my classmates to know."

Everyone in the circle was listening intently while mouths dropped open and eyes became locked on this majestic, little princess. I was puzzled, but found myself mesmerized with her tone of sincerity and confidence.

Before the closing school bell rang, Aaliyah got out one more fact. "I don't have any servants over here, but I'm learning to do things for myself. Most of the people we know do their own chores in this area."

The bell rang and for the first time in any Community Circle I've ever experienced, no one made a move to get up and out the door. This was the beginning of "tending court" which was held by Aaliyah Anippe, Egyptian Princess, in my ordinary, Third Grade classroom.

The second day of school Aaliyah arrived early. I said, "Good morning" as she walked into the room. She nodded her head and smiled. Returning the smile, I continued, "Aaliyah, since you are here early, why don't you choose where you would like to sit?"

She looked the room over and walked down an aisle to the back of the room to the middle desk. Sitting down, she began taking things out of her new book bag without another word. I returned to preparing my grade book.

It wasn't long before children were straggling in one by one. I seated each child from the chart I had made and wrote their names in the correct space. Within the next few minutes, our year began and we were off to a good start.

I'll skip the details of the first six weeks except to say we all learned a great deal about Egypt. Aaliyah had become a star student. By star, I don't mean the most outstanding student academically. She was the star as in someone who draws unusual attention due to their beauty, dress and gracious manners. Performer would be a good word here. It was as if each day Aaliyah had an inner-sense that switched on. Something that said, "Lights, Camera, Action" to her alone.

Anytime she moved to my desk or to the blackboard and back to her seat, the class seemed to stop as they followed her with eyes of wonder and awe. It wasn't long before I saw other little girls in the class begin to copy her way of speaking, her posture and her behavior. Soon I would have a whole classroom full of princesses!

Being truthful, this wasn't all bad. There wasn't a lot of whispering. The children remained in their seats unless called upon to walk to the blackboard. They were courteous to one another. Almost everyone arrived at school in a neat, well kept fashion.

The boys rough housed at recess, but began stopping by the boys bathroom to wash their face and hands on the way back to class. The girls made sure they were sitting up straight with well combed hair and fresh faces. They spoke softly when speaking and moved with the emulated style of Aaliyah. I was stunned by the influence one little girl could have on a classroom of children!

Way before mid-term, other teachers began dropping by my room for one reason or another. They remarked on the quiet atmosphere and politeness of my children when they had spoken with them on the playground. Civility was breaking out all over!

Mrs. Anippe was unable to make the first report card meeting. Aaliyah took her report card of straight A's home for her mother to sign. I received a note in return saying the she would be certain to make the next conference. It would be before she and Aaliyah had to return to Egypt.

The weeks flew by with my having one of the best classes of my career. Children were well behaved and part of a royal kingdom created on a small scale by Aaliyah Anippe. The second progress report period was almost upon us with more outstanding grades than the first six weeks. Manners had already become ingrained in most of my students. They were highly talked about throughout the school.

Checking my calendar, I saw that Mrs. Anippe was due at four o'clock on the last day of Teacher/Parent Conferences. She arrived on time and certainly wasn't anything I'd expected. She was short, a little overweight, and dressed conventionally with hair covered by a scarf. She was shy and appeared a bit nervous as she took a seat across from me. I began by telling her what a joy it had been to have Aaliyah in my class, even for a short time. Everyone was sad to hear they were returning to Egypt.

"Mrs. Gravett, I must start with a little family history and why we are here." Mrs. Anippe began. "My husband was in Egyptian Intelligence. When he was killed two years ago, Aaliyah was only six years old. It was a terrible experience for both of us. But, she refused to accept it. My husband, Ali, often disappeared for weeks at a time on one mission or another. We never knew where he was, or what country or on what kind of problem he was working."

"It was easy for Aaliyah to pretend he was on one of his missions and would return before too long. She was his little princess. He spent many evening hours telling her stories of princesses. He talked to her about how princesses dressed, walked and talked. He bought her every book going back into the centuries of long Egyptian royalty."

"He praised her when she behaved as if we were a royal family. We both smiled as she took on the airs of the royal princesses as in the history and story books. She wouldn't dress like the other little girls. She wanted beautiful dresses and outfits that stood out in a crowd. Ali babied her and had modified dresses of true royal princesses' clothing made for her."

"She began to be more and more like a fairy tale princess to me and was hardly ever out of character. Aaliyah and I were both trying to pick up the pieces of our lives and go
on. "

"I took her to a psychiatrist before we left Egypt. After several sessions, he told me that she was lovely and well behaved. He said the childhood fantasy wasn't harmful and that she would outgrow all the pretense and eventually accept her father's death. In the meantime, enjoy her beauty and impeccable style. He found her an intelligent child with her own special way of keeping sorrow out of her life for now."

Mrs. Anippe looked down, but not before I saw the tears in her eyes. "I should have told you earlier. I didn't believe she would continue all this in a new country, but she did. Please forgive me. We are here because Ali had papers that needed to be shared with American Intelligence. My husband's work is now complete. We'll return home to Egypt next week."

This is the story of a real girl, while I added the emphasis. I don't know anything about her life after she left to return to her home in Egypt. The reactions of the children to her while she was a part of our class were absolutely amazing. I decided not to tell the children the rest of Aaliyah's story.

There could probably be many adventures to write about what happened to Aaliyah after she left. While writing these memories, I recalled something she said during one of her first day's here when we talked about life in America and all the freedom we have in this country.

I want to talk about the Author/Writer- **George Thomas Whetter.** Tom is the author of numerous short stories. He tells of sitting on the floor next to the couch as his father, George, reads to him from a copy of *Children's Activities* magazine dated somewhere in the 1940's. He says those stories must have been what prompted him to become a story teller and finally a writer of short stories. Tom came by it naturally. The Whetter family migrated to Michigan's Upper Peninsula from Cornwall, England in the late 1800's. There wasn't much to do outside of the copper mines, other than eat pasties, play music and tell stories. Give him two words and he can make up some sort of story.

His story telling led him into a lifetime of sales; winning many awards for his work, among many other professional money making endeavors. He has a long list of jobs he held before finding his love of writing. He remarked to me that he knows a lot about a lot of things but not much about anything.

Tom currently writes a column for a local Lake City newspaper *The Missaukee Sentinel* called "Who Am I?" He designed the column because he didn't know one person before moving to Lake City from Kalamazoo in 2013. He felt it was a good way to meet people and to tell their story.

This book is dedicated to those who like to read and tell stories. That's what life is all about. We all have a story to tell.

George Thomas Whetter
G. Tom

SORRY, WRONG NUMBER

Ring-Ring-Ring

"99Th Street Credit Union. May I help you?"

"Hi honey. Boy I'm sure glad I got you. Do you have a minute to talk? Are you busy? Never mind. Just listen. I've got something really funny to tell you. Stop me if you get a customer or you have to go. You remember how high the grass got since the last hard rain? Well, I decided to mow. I got our new mower out of the shed, gassed it up and it started on the first pull. The kids had left the hose laying out in the backyard. They had been playing in the water spraying each other and of course they never put anything back. So I had to stop the mower. I tried to move the hose but it was heavy-full of water. It had been left turned on at the spigot and the sprayer nozzle was all clogged up with dirt. No water came out. I don't like leaving water in the hose in the hot sun. It ruins the hose and the grass when water gets so hot from the sun. I was peering into the opening of the sprayer when I turned the water off and back on. It poured out full blast. Of course it was steaming hot water. Unfortunately I was starring directly down into the sprayer as the water let loose and it sprayed dirt and hot water directly into my face. Now, I hate to go on with this story, since it becomes quite 'dirty.' You know the dirt that I told you about that was caked in the end of the sprayer? Well, when I smelled it, was not dirt! It was doggie poop! It sprayed all over me. You know how much I hate getting dog poop on my shoes? Then you can imagine how much I hate getting it on my face! At least the good thing was I only had my shorts and tee shirt on. My shoes will never be the same, however. After I shut down the water, I ran into the house kicking off my shoes. I hope you won't mind, but I couldn't help dripping all over our new kitchen tile. I know you will understand when I tell you the rest of my story. I tore off my socks and threw them on the washer along with my soggy, smelly, T shirt. I felt like kicking that Lab. He was all over me and wouldn't leave me alone. He kept humping my leg and saying with his look, 'Where did this character come from? He smells just like my poop! Boy, he needs a bath, bad!' I finally escaped the dog and was careful not to slip on the tile floor in the entryway. I was dripping poop and water all the way to the second floor. I just had to take a bath or at least a shower. I was afraid to lick my lips. Finally I got to the top of the stairs and grabbed one of your dog bath towels and decided to go to the third floor bathroom. I hadn't used that bathroom for a while, as you know, and as long as I had already waited this long, what difference could it make? Besides, I wasn't in the mood to wash down the walls of the shower and I know you would be angry with me if I didn't dry them off. I thought. I figured what you didn't know wouldn't hurt me. I wish we had finished that bathroom before, especially the flooring. I stepped on a couple of loose nails I had dropped and had not bothered to pick up previously. I didn't bleed, not much anyway, in case you wondered. I finally made it into the tub-shower and turned on the water while facing the sprayer so it would hit me directly in the face. I had to wash that stuff off my face as soon as I could. It was beginning to cake. I could hardly wait for the splash of hot water. It was going to feel sooo good! What do you think happened? The water came out of the sprayer in a slow dribble. I could spit faster than that. I think the problem was that I had left the hose in the back yard turned on full force and the water pressure to the third floor bathroom was not strong enough to put out more than a slow drizzle. I said a few choice words and determined that I had to get my body in some hot water. I left the third floor, stumbled down to the bedroom floor, and headed for the big bathroom. No, not the master bedroom bath, in case you wondered. I turned on the water and what a relief to have that sweet smelling H2O hit me in the face. I think I spent a half hour in there washing my body. What a relief to get that smell of dog poop off me. Isn't that funny?"

"What's that you said? Who is this?" Asked the surprised voice.

"Don't you know who this is? -- Who did I call anyway? -- Isn't this the 99th Street Credit Union?"

"Yes it is sir! To whom did you wish to speak? My name is Sue Smith. I'm the manager here at the bank."

Pause- Pause! "Do you know who this is?" I asked.

"NO- I have no idea- SIR!"

"Thank you! Good Bye!" CLICK!

LATER THAT DAY

"Hi Donna." I said. "How did your day go?" I looked up from the couch.

"Fine-fine." Donna said. "I'm glad it's Friday."

"Why's that?"

"Today was just one of those weird days."

"Why weird?'

"My boss got one of those strange telephone calls. There was some guy on the phone and he talked and he talked. She couldn't get a word in edgewise. She was upset because she thought it was an obscene phone call. She was so frazzled she left work early."

"Did she know who it was?"

"She wouldn't talk about it. How about you, Robert, did you get your yard work done?"

"Oh that! - I didn't do much." I said as I hiked my feet back up on the couch. "I just took it easy. It was too hot to mow."

Hair Brush

It happened twice a week. I would hear the knock at the back door of our two story bungalow. It wasn't the milkman placing the four quarts of milk in the milk shoot. I knew the sound of the milk box being opened and the clink of glass as the bottles slid through the open door of the milk shoot. I could tell the difference between full bottles and empties by the sound also.

I looked forward to the ice cold bottles of wonderful white stuff, capped with paper and the company logo stamped in red letters.

Sometimes I would steal into the house, when I forgot my key, by crawling in the milk box door. I was only eight years old, you understand.

I had better tell you now, what the sound was, before I get going again. It wasn't the knock of the milkman. The milkman didn't knock, but the Jewell Tea man did.

So it wasn't the milkman. Good! It was the Jewell Tea man that I was anxious to see. The Jewell Tea man also came to the back door. He would always knock on the wooden screen door. His knock always sounded the same. It was a distant type of knock. You know, a fast dot dot dot—-dot sound, three long and one short knocks.

Deliveries were never, never, made at the front door of our house, never! In fact, Mom would scold ME if my friends came to call my name "TOMMY" from the covered front porch.

"Do not have your friends come to the front door!" She would tell me. "Have them go to the back door!"

I was never allowed to touch the front door! I'll have to take that back. I was allowed to leave for school by the front door. Mom would kiss me and make sure I had tucked my scarf in and buttoned the top button of my "Pea" coat against my chin. I always hated that! I felt like a sausage. Plus I could smell bleach on her hands. She always did the laundry with bleach, Yuk!

"Tell your friends to go to the back door and knock. Do not have them yell!" She told me more than once."The neighbors complain. They are old and they sleep a lot."

They weren't, and they didn't. I knew them better than she did.

"OK Mom," I would say, not looking at her. I didn't think the kids would go to the back door, and they didn't. But I knew that by saying, "OK Mom," each time, that she would repeat the order and get some exercise cleaning out her lungs.

The boys would come into the front yard and yell my name, even after I told them not to. That was all right with me though. I did it at their homes too. As kids we knew everything about all the neighbors and the neighborhood. We knew the special hiding place where we could hide our fishing tackle. It was under the cobra bells.

At the first sign of spring we wanted to skip school to go fishing. The fishing spot was a mile or two away. We didn't care, we knew where we could swipe the sweetest cherries. Fences didn't mean too much to us, as we could hurdle them in one swift jump.

I was average size for my age of eight, and in the second grade at school. I was the hopscotch champ of the street, because of my long legs. And I was the fastest runner on the block. I used my fast running to my advantage when I was confronted by Jackie Moyer. Jackie was the block bully.

Mom made me dress proper for the forties. Nice long sleeved shirts in the fall and winter that were neatly washed in her wringer washer and pressed in her mangle iron machine. One time I was with her in the basement when she got her fingers caught in the wringer washer. There was a release button, but I was too scared to know which one to press. I didn't want to hurt her even more.

Mom saved her money for years to purchase that new washing machine. One time, while I was helping Mom push the machine full of water over to the floor drain, I pushed too hard. It tipped over and crashed on the basement floor chipping off three spots of the gleaming white porcelain. Those spots remained black thereafter.

Boys in the years of 1943-44 all wore knickers. One of my many Aunts, (everyone my Mother's age was called an Aunt), Aunt Lena, sewed my knickers out of an old wool coat. Everything in those days was recycled, especially clothing. I was so excited to have my own knickers, just like the big boys. I didn't even mind that the wool scratched my legs. When Aunt Lena noticed, she sewed a lining in the leg parts.

"How can I keep my pants from sliding down to my ankles?" I asked my Dad. He had worn knickers when he was a boy, as did all his brothers.

"Use rubber bands," he said.

Now rubber bands were in a limited supply back in those years. "There is a war on, you know." I heard that so many times, how could I forget? So anytime I could beg, borrow or steal a good rubber band I held on to it. These I placed just below my knees, over the top of my knickers to hold them up.

So for all fall and winter my legs looked like railroad tracks when I slid my rubber bands off my pants.

"Be careful not to break the bands!" Mom would say, "They are hard to find these days."

"Yes, I know Mother," as I placed them beside my RCA. radio on the top of the bookshelf, which Dad had made for me. On that same shelf I kept my favorite book, "*White Fang*" by Jack London. I liked that book so much I would limit my reading to only one page day, just so that I wouldn't finish the book too quickly.

Now, since rubber bands were so difficult to come by, I became very interested in the man I spoke about earlier. He was the Jewel Tea man. Mother would have him come to our home. She would purchase spices, cookbooks, sugar, almost anything that was difficult to buy at the corner store because of rationing and the war. I wasn't particularly interested in those other items, but I was interested in something he had.

When he came to the back door and Mom let him in, he would place his goodie carrier on the top step, just off the landing, three steps up. He took from his carrier a huge package of cards. My Mother's name and address was on one of those cards. When she would make an order he would write something down on the lines of the card with his short, stubby pencil. I remember his pencil had a great big eraser on the top. Ours were all chewed off. (My sister did it!) I would watch very closely as he slid a huge, thick, rubber band off the package of cards. That rubber band was the biggest I had ever seen!

"Boy," I said, "that's the biggest rubber band I have ever seen! I wish I had one like that." I looked straight at the rubber band and then directly at his face. He stood at my height cause he was at the landing level.

"I wish that I had an extra one," he said. "The company furnishes these rubber bands for the delivery salesmen and they are difficult to come by. There is a war on you know!"

"I know!" I said.

"I've had this one for a long while. They last for a long time if I take care of them," he said.

"Yeah," I said. I was very envious of his job and that he would have such a wondrous thing in his possession.

That day Mom felt like she would like to buy me something from the man, as I had been 'such a pest' by asking so many questions and such.

"What do you have in your carrier that would be something Tommy could use? I think he is at the age now where he should learn to brush his own hair."

She had picked up his larger, slick, paged catalog. It looked like a Sears and Roebuck catalog to me, except it didn't have the tissue paper in the middle. She was pointing at the picture of a brown curved handle of a Stanley hairbrush. "That would be perfect for him. I would like to order that."

I couldn't have been less interested. Now, if she had said she would buy me the rubber band, I would have been very happy but she didn't.

Two weeks later, right on schedule, the Jewel Tea man, whose name was John, arrived at the back door with his basket of goodies. Mom and I met him at his knock and I opened the door before Mom could get there. Setting his basket of goodies down on the top step, as he always did, he reached into his basket and pulled out that packet of cards with the beautiful rubber band attached.

Holding it in his left hand, he used his right to reach into the basket to pull out a small box. It was pleasantly wrapped with pretty paper and held closed with a brand new yellow rubber band! It was just like the one that held the cards together.

I could hardly believe it! I had my very own rubber band! I kept thinking of all the ways the I could use it. Then I slowly unwrapped the small box and inside was the most beautiful hairbrush I had ever seen. It even had genuine nylon bristles. I thought that was kinda special since the only time I ever heard that word 'nylon' referred to what ladies wore on their legs. I would hear them complain about their nylon stockings, almost crying, "Damn! I have a run in my nylon!"

Disaster, I thought when listening to this, *what's all the fuss about? It must be the end of the world!*

During the workday my Mom and the guy's moms wore dresses and bobby socks that were pushed down around the ankles. Mom wore an apron to protect her dress, as she spent most of her day in the kitchen making and preparing meals.

I never thought that she was very attractive until she got dressed up on Friday evenings. She would put on her nylon stockings and then my Dad, sister and I would go out to dinner and a movie at the Western Theatre.

I never had a hairbrush before. My Mom used a comb on my hair only once a day, or after my bath. I practiced and practiced brushing my hair. It was quite curly in those days. Watching myself in the mirror was interesting, as I remember. Everything was backward as seen in the mirror from what it really was. I had to get used to the part on the opposite side of my head from which I thought it was.

Over time the brush bristles began to fill in with broken off hair. I wondered, how do I get the hair out of the brush? I decided to burn it out. I very quietly snuck down to the kitchen where I 'borrowed' two wooden matches. Mother had them in a little metal container kept over the gas cook stove.

Don't worry, I thought, *she didn't see me take them and she won't miss them.*

I left the kitchen and ascended the stairs to my bedroom. I carefully sat down at my desk and struck a match. The hair in my new brush, after several weeks of use, was completely matted in the bristles of the brush. I carefully turned the brush over so that the bristles were in the down position. Then I moved the burning match to the brush to light the hair.

I didn't want to take too long or else I would change my mind. As I moved the flame to the hair the bright flame ignited the hair into heavy flames.

I was too young to know all the swear words in the world, but as it burst into flames it startled me so, and almost singed my own black curly hair. All the four letter words that I had never heard came roaring out of my mouth.

Now panic set in! I sat there with this burning torch in my hand. I was afraid that I was about to burn the house down. The bathroom was too far away and all I could think of was to blow on the burning hair. So, I blew and I blew until I was faint and out of breath. Finally the hair that had been ignited totally burned up. I set the smoldering hot hairbrush down on my desk. My hands were shaking so badly that I was afraid that I would drop it on the floor.

Did I ruin my brush? How would I tell my mother the next time she saw my brush? These questions drifted in and out of my head as I sat there in wonderment.

It took me several days to talk to my sister about my experience. I usually only told her about things that I didn't want to talk to my parents about. I only told her because I felt that I needed an ally. Sometimes I wished that I hadn't told her my secrets for fear that she would tell on me. But to my knowledge, she never did.

She was two years my senior. Her name was Patty, or Pat as her friends call her. The boys thought she was really pretty with her long, curly, black hair. She giggled a lot when they said things to her. Sometimes she would get angry with me and tell me to go away, right in front of her boyfriends. When all the time I thought that they came to see me! She had a lot of boyfriends. That was why the boys spent so much time coming to our house and calling MY name. Some of them didn't really want me; they wanted to see Patty!

After hearing my story about almost burning up the house, she suggested that I could have used a steel hairbrush cleaner to clean out my brush. Well, I didn't know that there was such a thing.

My hairbrush, to this date, is sixty-two years old. I use it practically every day. There are several bristles missing, thirty or forty, right in the middle of the brush. Some of the remaining bristles are bent sideways reminding me of that particular day many years ago.

I've often thought of purchasing a new brush to replace it. Then the first question that comes to my mind is: What would I do with my old one? I couldn't stand to part with that old brush. I have too many memories. Besides, at this age what else do I have that I treasure as much, after all these years?

The problem was solved this past year. I feel really good about my decision. I attended a flea market, not very far from my new cottage, and accidentally on purpose, found a booth that sold Stanley hair brushes. I couldn't help myself! I opened my wallet and forked over a large sum of money to purchase a brand new hairbrush, just like my old one. The only difference was the it was not in a box wrapped with a yellow rubber band.

I don't feel too bad, either, since I now have two homes. Our home in the city and a cottage in the woods. I now have a hairbrush in each place. Which one did I take to the woods? I'm sure you would want to know!

Now, I have a very important question to ask you. If you had a special hairbrush that old, which hairbrush would YOU take to the woods?

Do you have a favorite hairbrush? Do you care? I did! I do! You might say that this is a simple story and it is! But it is true. But then, all MY stories are true!

P.S. Just one more thing before you leave me. Since there is not much hair left up there, what do I need a hairbrush for anyway? My barber tells me he charges more just to find a hair to cut.

Yours truly,
Tommy

My Brothers and Me

I have three brothers. We decided to build us a house, well not together, but one for each of us. Mine, I knew, would be the best.

All three of us look alike, except I am the most handsome. It's because I wear blue breeches. You can tell us apart that way.

We are all supposed to build our own house. I like to do things fast, so I helped my Purple Pants Brother build his house out of straw. We built it fast and if the breath of the Big Bad Wolf should blow his house down so he could scare him, so what! He can just build another one just as easy. Why waste the time?

My second brother is dressed in yellow. He is even lazier than Purple Pants, and wants to get his house build fast! Not as fast as me and Purple Pants, however, and his house is not as pretty as mine is gonna be. But he got finished in a hurry so the he could dance and sing with Purple Pants.

They sing songs. The songs go like this, "We built our houses and houses today, my brother Purple Pants and Me. My brother Yellow Pants and me. Mine is the best, because it's made of straw. Its cozy and soft and it's beautiful too."

My Yellow Pants Brother sang: "My house is made of sticks and it's stronger than yours, Tra-la- Tra-la-Tra-la-la-la."

They are kind-a stupid songs, wouldn't you agree? But if they play a flute and a violin along, then they don't sound quite so bad. My brothers are terrible dancers, especially when they sing and dance around with no pants on.

My third brother, oh thats me! I wear Blue Overalls. I don't just wear a shirt. Not just a top like some other cartoon characters. That's so you can identify me from my brothers.

I built my house out of bricks. I have no idea where they came from, that's just part of the story. Oh well, perhaps I got them from out in the middle of the woods someplace place? I said I wanted to build my house strong so it couldn't be blown down.

My brothers thought they could build ten houses in the time it took me to build one. It took so long making mortar and slapping it on that I had no time to play, dance or sing and play music with them. What a shame, besides, I think I was the smartest one of us because my house was made of brick.

I enjoyed rubbing in it. As I worked I would say that I did not have the time to play. I said that work and play don't mix. Boy, was I wrong!

Now, out in the woods there lived a Big Bad Wolf! I never knew why he was called the "Big Bad Wolf." Mom called him that. How would she know? Had she ever met him? Personally?

Old Wolfe was not at all dressed very classy in his little red hat and his shirtless bib overalls. At least he wore pants! He had a real nice voice. He liked to sing, "Who's afraid of the Big Bad Wolf, the Big Bad Wolf? The Big Bad Wolf? Who's afraid of the Big Bad Wolf, Tra la la laaaa!"

He liked to scare the heck out of us. He doesn't scare me though. But he does have big teeth. When he came to my house I just stepped in and closed the door. He huffed and he puffed and he tried to blow my house in. I have to admit he really has bad breath! I wondered what he had eaten that day. Not a pig like me, I hope. I would taste really good.

I knew I could build a house really strong. I also knew I could just take off running and he couldn't catch me. I'm pretty fast at running, as well as good looking.

Then the wolf went to my second brother's house made of sticks. My brother saw what he tried to do to my house, so he ran inside and slammed the door. The wolf blew and he blew and he blew the stick house in. Old Yellow Pants knew that he couldn't out run the wolf so he subjected himself to the wolf's wants and desires. He signed on to be his butler. He even promised to take care of Old Wolfe, to do his dishes and sweep his floor and such. Boy, what a bore. He won't get paid for it either!

Now the wolf is really hungry, and he's mad! He can't catch me and he needed another butler now. And he needs to eat, after all, he is a wolf that eats pigs! So he huffed and he puffed and he huffed and he puffed again, but he couldn't blow my brick house in.

"What——(hell)——(whoops). What the heck is wrong?" He said out loud so we could all hear him. He couldn't blow my house down no matter how hard he blew.

Do you know what he did then? I'll tell you what! He gave up. He called me, the Blue Brother, and asked if he could move in with me because I had such a nice house. He would be much happier to have a strong house like mine to live in. He said he had a butler now, my Yellow Brother, to do all the work. He promised to eat only strawberries and honey. He said he would send Old Yellow Pants out to gather them to eat.

"Such a deal!" I thought.

My Purple Pants brother makes me laugh when he says his straw house is better than mine! Old Wolfy would come over once in a while and practice blowing down his house. He didn't care, he could just build another one. Thats what he told me, because that way he wouldn't have to sweep the floor.

And everyone is happy.

The end.

P.S. This is my story. I am the Blue Pants Pig and it's my version of the story, *"Three Little Pigs."* My story makes more sense to me.

Made in the USA
Lexington, KY
13 April 2018